Praise for *The Pattern Future*

"A rare book written by a rare polymath, a book filled with amazing stories on Mark Anderson's most stunning intellectual trajectory—from the world of discovering the patterns that lie beneath complexity mathematics and the mysteries of relativity theory to uncovering the patterns driving many aspects of global trade and currency wars.

"Patterns matter now more than ever, and developing the skill to find them is getting harder and harder, as complexity theory now seems to underlie so much of our world, best understood as comprising many kinds of interacting flows.

"Reading this book will give us all insight into how a master continues to do this year after year after year."

> —John Seely Brown, independent co-chairman of Deloitte's Center for the Edge, former chief scientist of Xerox Corp., and former director of the Xerox Palo Alto Research Center (PARC)

"Our brains appear to be massive pattern matchers, according to recent neural studies. Some brains seem to match patterns better than others, and Mark Anderson's works especially well, as he explains in this wide-ranging book."

> —Vint Cerf, internet pioneer and VP/chief internet evangelist of Google

"In *The Pattern Future*, Mark Anderson gives us a mini-biography illustrating his uncanny ability to discern patterns, whether in economics, science, education, or innovation. But Mark goes further and provides compelling examples of how the knowledge one gains from recognizing pattern shifts requires high moral courage to act on those insights, when everyone else is blind to the drastic change about to happen. The combination of understanding how to see patterns and the courage to act on their implications gives Mark his extraordinary Superpower. Quite a remarkable story!"

> —Larry Smarr, founding director of the California Institute for Telecommunications and Information Technology (Calit2, a UC San Diego/UC Irvine partnership)

"Mark R. Anderson has produced a brilliant and deeply insightful account of correlating pattern recognition of present and past events with prediction of future events. Such knowledge is important to grasp as we sit on the threshold of explosive progress in machine learning."

> —Dan Goldin, president and CEO of KnuEdge and past administrator of NASA

"The most breathtaking prediction I have heard was a mystic in the Himalayas who predicted that smallpox would be eradicated 'soon.' This was in the middle of the raging epidemic afflicting more than 250,000 in India in 1973, when hardly anyone thought the disease could be contained, let alone eradicated. That mystic was my teacher, Neem Karoli Baba, and I was sitting there when he made that prediction, and I remained in South Asia to see the last case of killer smallpox in nature in Bangladesh only a few years later. I don't know if that should be called prediction or prophecy, nor if it was based on scientific logic or mystical insight, nor if it was pattern matching or magic, but it came true just as he foresaw, and that was stunning.

"The second most stunning prediction—or rather, family of predictions—I have seen were at Mark Anderson's FiRe (Future in Review) conferences. Mark is not a religious mystic, but sometimes I think he might as well be, for how well he seems to 'see' the future. Now he has written a book compiling some of his secrets and tools and methods and insights, how he 'sees' the future.

"Not many have prophetic powers, but all of us can learn a lot about the science and art of prediction by studying this book, reading about the tools Mark has made accessible to those of us who are mere mortals. For those of us who are struggling to make sense of the present and peer into the future, the methods Mark reveals in *The Pattern Future* are a gift!"

—Dr. Larry Brilliant, chair of the Skoll Global Threats Fund and author of *Sometimes Brilliant*

"In a career where I've been lucky enough to meet many of the best of the brightest, Mark is the smartest person in the world I've met who's still alive."

—William Lohse, venture capitalist and founder of Social Starts LP and Pivot Conference

"Mark Anderson's reputation as a trend predictor is well-established, and with *The Pattern Future*, he unveils how he does it. I found the techniques and stories to be useful for those who are anticipating and planning for the future."

—Paul Daugherty, chief technology and innovation officer of Accenture

"Mark Anderson has earned his reputation as an extraordinarily prescient predictor of the unanticipated. His focus is on patterns as they persist through time and, critically, the subtle indications that what has been an established pattern is subject to more or less radical change. He now shares his distinctive approach to reading the future from the observable past and present."

—Bill Janeway, senior advisor at Warburg Pincus and faculty of Economics at the University of Cambridge

THE
PATTERN
FUTURE

THE
PATTERN
FUTURE

FINDING THE WORLD'S GREAT SECRETS AND PREDICTING THE FUTURE USING PATTERN DISCOVERY

MARK R. ANDERSON

FOREWORD BY DAVID BRIN

PUBLISHED IN THE UNITED STATES OF AMERICA BY

A DIVISION OF STRATEGIC NEWS SERVICE LLC

Published in the United States of America by FiReBooks, a division of the Strategic News Service.
P.O. Box 1969
Friday Harbor, Washington 98250
www.stratnews.com

FiRe, FiReBooks, and Strategic News Service (SNS) are registered international trademarks. All other trademarks, servicemarks, registered trademarks, and registered servicemarks are the property of their respective owners.

Ordering Information:
Bookstores and wholesalers should contact the publisher at the address above. Special discounts are available on quantity purchases by corporations, associations, and others. For details, contact the publisher. The publisher is not responsible for websites (or their content) that are not owned by the publisher.

Cover photo © Sally L. Anderson, Canal du Midi

ISBN (paperback): 978-0-9967254-4-6
ISBN (hardback): 978-0-9967254-5-3
ISBN (ebook): 978-0-9967254-3-9

10 9 8 7 6 5 4 3 2 1

Printed in the United States of America

Contents

Part 3
Using Patterns to Predict (and Perhaps Improve) the Future

Part 4
Analyzing the Patterns Behind Three Major Calls

Foreword

Anticipation.

It's the most uniquely human trait, peering at a future that doesn't yet exist, except in two wispy little nubs of gray matter, just above the eyes. Those prefrontal lobes are – to crib from the Bible – "lamps on the brow" that empower us to concoct what-if scenarios about the territory ahead. It must have conferred advantages on our ancestors, because we've spent a lot of time and energy making up stories about days and hours to come. These ranged from mere daydreams to the auguries and ravings of prophets, to stock market gambling, all the way to science fiction.

Our sincere civil servants in all those alphabet agencies – and officers of any company – know that anticipation is their topmost job. When you get it right, you can act to stanch threats, grab opportunities, and open paths for initiative. Hence, nowadays your corporate CEO or head of an intelligence agency allocates plenty of money and effort to both data collection and predictive models. Some efforts have yielded fascinating results, as in recent appraisals of "amateur wisdom" by the Intelligence Advanced Research Projects Agency (IARPA). And yes, that includes bringing in science-fiction authors to poke and slash at the walls of the predictive box.

For years, I harangued leaders in both commerce and government that they should focus on a simple project: *Find ways to track who's right a lot!* And which pompous seers more often get it wrong, offering metrics to a public that's desperately beset by charismatic charlatans. But above all, find those who are *good* at looking ahead.

Study them. Decipher their methods. More often than not, they're happy to teach.

Which brings us to Mark Anderson. As is almost always the case, Mark was way ahead of me in this, pioneering methods of self-tracking and making his own forecasts easy to score. And why wouldn't he? When you're on-target as often as he's been, you'll naturally want people to see clear results. Some of my fans and readers keep a wiki to track predictions from my novels and speeches, but Mark is tracked by some of the fiercest ands most-accomplished women and men in our civilization.

This book is about how he does what he does. At the Strategic News Service, Mark and his analysts use their newsletter to peel back surfaces, looking for the trends under trends. He travels the world, invited by sages and leaders who ask "*What did we miss?*" The annual Future in Review – or *FiRe* – conference is one of the best and most lively events of its kind, bringing together a growing community of tech business leaders and other innovators, exploring what's next. A number of fast-rising companies got their crucial boost after being chosen as "FiReStarters," and the associated FiReFilms documentary film movement has widespread influence. Each year's FiRe CTO Design Challenge pits a few dozen top minds against some intractable problem – and generally all obstacles topple in just 48 hours. Ably augmented by both the Anderson clan and this growing community, Mark has put one priority above all others – fostering creative problem-solving.

And now he's sharing his core methods with you. Mark didn't have to invent any arm-waved terminology; the key words were already there – *pattern recognition*. Indeed, AI researchers have poured billions into teaching our machines to parse things like picking out a dog amid cats. But Mark is after much subtler configurations – patterns of cause and effect that still pop out only when they are sought by human minds. Minds who are simultaneously both open and critical.

In the autobiographical sections of this book, you'll murmur, "Sure, Mark Anderson was raised for this! But what chance have *I* to gain such pattern-seeking mastery?" But read on. He'll offer you dozens of tools, rooted in real-world examples. And that *stretching* sensation you'll feel – just above the eyes – will be your anticipatory muscles – those prefrontal lobes – pumping up!

Eager to get on with it? Well, let me keep you for one further thought.

Mark talks about many things that can block accurate pattern recognition. One of the worst of these is our human propensity for delusion. Imagination can be our greatest gift, when it's harnessed to enhance creativity. But those subjective colors, concepts, dogmas, expectations, grudges, and wish-fantasies that we overlay upon the world can also lead to misperception and error. Massively shared delusions have sometimes produced hells on Earth. The best cure has been something we usually deem bitter medicine – criticism. It works because other people have their own delusions, but they don't share yours. Moreover, both friends and enemies will happily point out your delusions. And you'll return the favor, pointing out theirs.

It is the reciprocality of criticism – in markets, democracy, science, and other adversarial arenas – that I believe unleashed us, allowing many to start seeing patterns that might be true *whether they liked it or not.*

Here lies the reason (I think) that Mark Anderson left the serene towers of science to apply his pattern-seeking gifts in the spuming currents of commerce. Science already is comfortable with reciprocal delusion piercing. But out there in our wild markets, where cheating and self-deception abound, is also where humanity builds and allocates the vast wealth we need, to end poverty and injustice, to solve problems and reach for the stars. Out there in the messy souks and bazaars of capital and policy . . . that is where we desperately need better pattern recognition, by officers of the state, by leaders of companies, and especially by average citizens. We must get better at perceiving patterns in the way that others (and that person in the mirror) are both wrong and right.

Here's a toolkit to get started.

David Brin
Author and Physicist
Encinitas, California, October 2017

Introduction

It is possible to have no formal education in a subject, yet be able to make critical discoveries in that area – discoveries that can change the world. This ability is the result of seeing patterns with an objective clarity and precision that often elude even those recognized as experts in their fields. It turns out that seeing such patterns in the present leads directly – and provably – to being able to project them into the future, and to making consistently accurate predictions.

How can you discover things you have no "right" to know, in fields in which you have no training – and then share this knowledge with global experts? How can you use these discoveries – and the friendships, relationships, and alliances that grow from them – to try turning our future a few degrees toward more positive, optimistic paths?

As a result of my success in this work, I've had the privilege of briefing corporate CEOs and other executives, as well as a number of agencies. In the US, these include the White House, the Department of State, the Department of Justice, the NSA, the CIA, the FBI, the NGA, the USTR, and the DHS. In Australia, past and present prime ministers and the minister for the Department of Broadband, Communications, and the Digital Economy. In the UK, the heads of GCHQ, MI5, MI6, the Cabinet office minister, and the BIS. And in other parts of the world, leaders in high office in Sweden, Germany, and Iceland.

The use of pattern recognition can lead a person who lacks professional training to a level of discovery and understanding that even world leaders find useful. My hope is that this book will provide an incentive for others to take up the practice of using pattern recognition, and the related practice of pattern discovery, as critically important tools in both seeing the present more clearly and accurately predicting the future.

This book also includes descriptions of my personal experiences as I've discovered the powers and practical uses of pattern recognition and its application to many disparate subject areas. Using these tools, I've been able to make accurate predictions (and effect a small amount of change, as well as contribute new theories) in physics, genetics, medicine, technology, finance, and the global economy. The result has been a success rate of 94.7% in publicly evaluated predictions over 22 years. In other words, pattern recognition leads to a better understanding of what's happening now – which leads to new theories of *how* things happen – and to a better understanding of what will happen next.

How was I, with no formal training in finance or economics, able to publicly predict both the Global Financial Collapse (GFC) of 2007/2008 and the Oil Price Collapse of 2014/2015? The answer is simple: I was studying pattern recognition rather than the opinions of the financial and economic experts of the day. These two events are arguably the most important economic events of our lifetime. Of the first, the *Financial Times* has said that not a single trained economist predicted the GFC[1] (although many afterward claimed to have done so); of the second, Saudi Prince Alwaleed bin Talal said: "No one anticipated it was going to happen. Anyone who says they anticipated this 50% drop [in price] is not saying the truth."[2]

Welcome to the power of pattern recognition.

---

[1] Chris Giles, "The Economic Forecasters' Failing Vision," *Financial Times* (Nov. 28, 2009), https://www.ft.com/content/50007754-ca35-11dd-93e5-000077b07658.

[2] Maria Bartiromo, "Saudi Prince: $100-a-Barrel Oil 'Never' Again," *USA Today* (Jan. 11, 2015), https://www.usatoday.com/story/money/columnist/bartiromo/2015/01/11/bartiromo-saudi-prince-alwaleed-oil-100-barrel/21484911/.

Through this book, I hope to share the incredible excitement of finding a new way of seeing patterns in the present, and by doing so to provide a basic guide on how to use these new insights to accurately predict related future events.

Finally, it is as important to state what this book is *not*: It is neither a scientific text on the field of pattern recognition nor a deep dive into any of the subject areas addressed – although, as cofounder of the new Pattern Recognition Laboratory at UC San Diego, I plan to write about these topics in the future.

Mark Anderson
Friday Harbor, Washington, October 2017

Part 1

Seeing Patterns

Chapter 1

Building a Pattern Recognition Brain

People used to ask me whether making accurate predictions was really possible, but I've found, after having done it successfully – and publicly – for over 20 years, that today the most common question is *How* do you do it?

We've learned recently that the brain, regardless of age, is much more plastic than we'd previously thought.[1] So it should not be news to anyone interested in prediction to know that it helps to start with your own brain.

What are the key attributes we're looking for, and how can we adjust our brains to be more effective in these areas?

Pattern recognition, and what I call "pattern resolution," are core to the process.

Pattern Recognition, Discovery, and Resolution

The definition of *pattern recognition* is obvious: our brains notice repetition in similarities or differences among things. *Pattern discovery* is the process of finding unique and important new patterns

---

[1] Norman Doidge, *The Brain That Changes Itself: Stories of Personal Triumph from the Frontiers of Brain Science* (New York: Penguin Books, 2007).

not seen before. And *pattern resolution* is what our brains *do* when
we see a pattern made or a pattern broken. Is what we're seeing part
of a larger pattern, or should it get our attention because it breaks
from expected patterns? If I start to play a musical scale and then
stop abruptly, someone listening can easily fill in the next tone.
Just as clearly, if I play a major scale and then throw in a (wrong)
half-tone, the mistake is clear right off, even to the untrained ear.
If I make the same mistake several times, the listener recognizes
that it's part of a larger pattern, and we might both hear it as a new
musical scale.

To a large degree, the difference between what we perceive as
"noise" and what we perceive as "music" comes down to our brain's
ability to detect patterns within repeated sounds.

I'm using music as an example not because it's the only apt met-
aphor, but because music itself is really nothing but mathematical
patterns put to sound. There is something deeply fascinating about
how we respond to music, to these mathematical patterns, that may
actually reach into the structure of the human brain.

Here is an eerie example: A C-major chord is made of perfect
(and even) mathematical intervals; it's pure math. If I play a C-major
chord followed by a C-minor chord to a room filled with people
from most countries in the world, virtually all of them will say that
the first sounds "happy" and the second sounds "sad." (Someday,
someone will probably get a Nobel Prize for explaining this hard-
wired connection between mathematical patterns and near-universal
human emotions.)

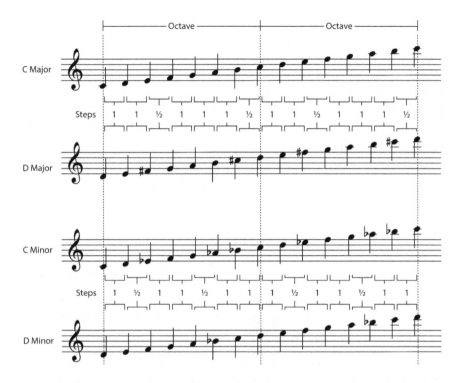

Figure 1-1. Two types of musical scales – major and minor. All major scales, regardless of key, show the same mathematical pattern of intervals – one that any listener would immediately recognize. Similarly, all minor scales share with one another the same mathematical pattern of intervals. Any note left out would create an uneven jump, or a "pattern broken," equally evident to any observer.

If *"How* do you do it?" is the most common question I'm asked, the second most common question is: "What can I do to improve my pattern recognition abilities and my ability to see the world around me, solve big problems, and predict future events?"

Admittedly, it helps to start early, when our brains – our biocomputers – are under construction.

My Family's Way

When my parents moved to our (then) small Illinois town of Elmhurst, my maternal grandparents moved there at the same time. No doubt this happens in many families, but in our case, I've always believed that my grandmother was focused, even then, on becoming the most amazing teacher in my young life.

She began with the Socratic method, asking why I thought the planets circled the sun, or why the owl's head turned nearly all the way around. She taught me to read by attaching musical tones (a hard-wired pattern) to all of the vowels (a pattern I was trying to learn), and then called me on the phone every morning to get me to repeat them: a, e, i, o, u (up and down a musical scale); ba, be, bi, bo, bu; and so on. Today, scientists have found evidence that this *exact* technique is far more successful in teaching reading than is rote memorization.

Next came physical puzzles – shapes, colors, fits, geometries – all in different games and challenges that forced my brain to think in terms of patterns. Those familiar with Piaget's work will recognize his finding that adding patterns to preferred learning modes appears to help create a brain that sees patterns more readily.

A bit later, the physical puzzles became more complex: "What makes this clock work?" Or – my version – "What happens when you lock the bathroom door from the inside and then take the lock apart?" (Nothing good.)

These exercises were soon followed by intellectual puzzles. "Why do you think the leaves are green?" my grandmother would ask me. What makes the wind blow? How do the cicadas make that interesting sound?

In retrospect, I have no doubt that my grandmother was intentionally going about the process of building her idea of the perfect pattern-matching brain – although she wouldn't have called it that – and that she recognized the importance of instilling curiosity in the young mind. You can't become a pattern master if you aren't curious about patterns.

Research shows us that the wiring in the young brain is directly affected by the patterns available in the brain's environment, and that the development process includes massive over-wiring in the first years, followed later on by pruning back what's not needed. In fact, kittens raised in an all–vertical-stripe environment can't see horizontal stripes; their brains haven't been exposed to this opposite pattern.[2,3]

| Birth | 5 Years | 14 Years |

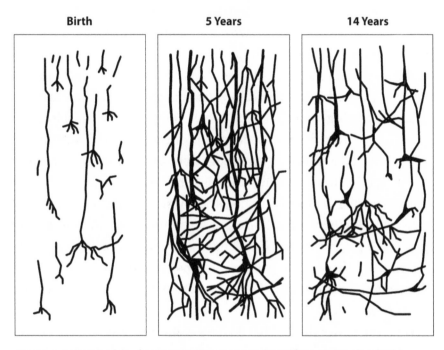

Figure 1-2. Brain neural development over time. Image adapted from J. LeRoy Conel's The Postnatal Development of the Human Cerebral Cortex. *Cambridge, MA: Harvard University Press, 1959.*

---

[2] Dorothy G. Flood and Paul D. Coleman, "Demonstration of Orientation Columns with [^{14}C]2-deoxyglucose in a Cat Reared in a Striped Environment," *Brain Research*, 173:3, Sept. 21, 1979: 538–542.

[3] Frank Sengpiel, Petra Stawinski, and Tobias Bonhoeffer, "Influence of Experience on Orientation Maps in Cat Visual Cortex," *Nature Neuroscience* 2, 727–732 (1999), doi:10.1038/11192.

Research also shows visual patterns directly represented in brain activity, literally transcribed from the outside world into the visual cortex, through the eye. Clearly, visual patterns from the outside world can be mapped to activate, and affect, brain structure. This is also true, I believe, for the patterns of sound, as noted above.

Because my grandmother had spent her youth preparing for a career as a concert pianist, I was surrounded by live performances of Bach, Schumann, Schubert, Chopin, and many other classical composers, no doubt from before the day of my birth.

This may well be the best way to design a pattern-based biocomputer – by exposing the brain to classical music from the beginning. While there remains some debate about the "Mozart Effect" in children and the effect of classical music on test-takers of an older age, here I'm talking about creating increasingly pattern-capable brain structures during the early years of life. There is a significant amount of scientific data showing that brain-structure changes are elicited by listening to patterned sounds, as well as by seeing images.[4]

Recognizing patterns may be the most important first line of defense in seeing the world clearly, but training for the subsequent process of pattern resolution is equally important. Being able to see (or hear, or otherwise notice) the patterns around us is a critical skill, but seeing a "pattern made" or a "pattern broken" isn't of much use on its own.

Once we notice them, what do these patterns mean?

My father was an engineer, and his contribution to building a young biocomputer was to expose me to science, both hands-on and through reading, and to physically build things with me in his basement shop. While I devoured each copy of a long series of magazines on all the sciences as they came in the mail, I also pored over his

[4] Hans Menning, Larry E. Roberts, and Christo Pantev, "Plastic Changes in the Auditory Cortex Induced by Intensive Frequency Discrimination Training," *Neuroreport*, 11:4, 817–822 (2000).

Aviation Week as each copy arrived. Before long, he started finding me books on advanced science and mathematics, such as George Gamow's *One Two Three . . . Infinity.*

My father had the insight to feed my love of chemistry with several basement labs of my own. Better still, he introduced me to a friend of his who was a professional chemist. This friend had a massive basement laboratory, an underground fallout shelter with a hole in the door for a gun muzzle, and a sabre scar on his cheek. Wow!

On weekends my father and I built and fired off rockets in the schoolyard, and we created a lifelike copy of the Cape Canaveral launch site to scale. Science – the study of what is true, and how things work – took over my consciousness, and my young biocomputer became adept at connecting things with ideas, including why rockets blow up.

Research has clearly shown that there are distinct stages of brain development, beginning at birth; and further shown, as mentioned earlier, that older brains are more plastic than previously thought. My experience, which might seem strange to some, was that this staging led to a series of "refresh" requirements in building my own biocomputer, intentionally exposing myself to huge new sets of patterns. For example, at 14, after the culture shock of a first summer in Europe (and falling in love with a much older French girl), I spent a year talking to almost no one, wearing a single set of clothes, and listening to a different piece of classical music from our local library each day.

My musical goal was to hear it all, every piece, by every composer in the collection. This turned out to serve as training for my now-older brain, having occurred just when my biocomputer was supposed to be "paring back" from the massive nerve count present in the majority of 14-year-olds (see Figure 1-2 on page 11). What happens if that biocomputer undergoes sustained exposure to classical music just when it's deciding what to edit out? I don't know the science behind this, but my guess is that the pattern-recognition structures are kept, and are probably refined.

A year later, I decided that I needed to read every title in the "Great Books" section of the best local bookstore, and came pretty close to doing so. I was interested in literature, but I had another motive in this hunt: the classics are, if nothing else, great descriptions of the many patterns of human behavior. If we want a biocomputer to be able to recognize human patterns, it needs to know what they are – although I would've described my curiosity differently at the time.

A Turning Point . . . and Back to Square One

All of this brain preparation appeared to be working: I was salutatorian at my high school, went to Stanford and took two degrees in four years, and moved on to a PhD program in a new scientific field under a brilliant young professor. It was in my second year at the University of British Columbia that I realized I'd made a couple of major mistakes. First, I had trained myself for much broader, if not deeper, studies than normal science research would allow. Second, and perhaps more important, my blunt personality was not well-suited to the politics of the university, despite the years I had spent there.

Although I'd been focused on science until that moment, it suddenly occurred to me that there might be things even more difficult, more intellectually challenging, and more exciting, to explore. I quit the PhD program and moved to a small island in Washington state. And there I waited for the next big idea to strike.

One morning, I found myself standing in a bookstore, looking out over the bay. Almost as if in a dream, I suddenly realized that pattern recognition was the most important aspect of training the brain, and I needed to start applying this process from scratch.

Looking back, I'm not sure that before that moment I'd ever

consciously thought about pattern recognition. I would have to start learning all over again, seeing the world in a new way.

So I did.

My hope, at the time, was to find a new way of understanding what the world was made of and how it worked. It hadn't occurred to me that I was setting myself on a path of predicting the future.

For the next few years, I applied pattern recognition and discovery to the most difficult tasks I could find, starting with the place where Einstein had gotten stuck in theoretical physics. I knew the only way I would have any chance of success lay in finding the answer to one question: Had I really found a new way of seeing the world?

I have no doubt that there is a nearly infinite number of ways to build a brain that is good or great at pattern recognition. By sharing my experiences, I'm not in any way implying that these are the only, or even the best, means to do so; rather, I hope this laying-out of at least one set of principles, to which I can personally attest, inspires others to look for their own ways, regardless of current wisdom in science.

Chapter 2

Learning to See:
Dropping Our Frames

I was attending a reception on the lawn of the Australian ambassador to the United States as a member of the Australian American Leadership Dialogue. It had been a busy day in Washington, DC, with meetings at the White House and with a number of K Street lobbyist groups, followed by unwinding at a reception and dinner. Everyone in this group was a leader of some kind, from Nobel scientists to global mining executives.

Sometimes things come together all at once. It's as though a host of ideas has been waiting in the mind's anteroom, and suddenly all push through in one Aha! moment. That's how it was for me on that sunny afternoon.

For years, a big problem had been puzzling me: people did not seem to be able to see the world around them. This wasn't always a symptom of political or emotional or even religious bias: one scientific study[1] has even shown that fully one-half of subjects do not see, for instance, a gorilla on a basketball court, if there's a diversion, such as fast play or a simultaneous assigned task.

---

[1] Daniel J. Simons and Christopher F. Chabris, "Gorillas in Our Midst: Sustained Inattentional Blindness for Dynamic Events," *Perception*, 28:9, 1059–1074.

Worse, it appeared to me that the human brain blocks out detail in order to be more efficient. Theoretically, or perhaps in ancient days, this may have been a brilliant strategy. But in modern times, it has led to radically different perceptions of the world and how it works. People argue not just about their opinions of the world; *they are often really seeing different worlds.*

Knowing this, how can anyone have *any* kind of functional conversation with anyone else? After all, like the dog in Gary Larson's *Far Side* cartoon that hears only her own name in the sea of her owner's words, people seem to be selective listeners, hearing only what they're listening for, or already believe.

Perhaps none of us is really communicating at all. Is it possible that the basic state of affairs is that each of us is a perception world all to ourselves, with each one of the worlds around us as different and unique as our biases? Because our views of the world are filtered by our beliefs – even in the cause of mental efficiency – the result is a near certainty that none of us can communicate effectively.

Of course, I had no hard evidence for my extrapolations.

On this day, at the party on the lawn, I found myself in conversation with one of the world's leading neurologists, Dr. Graeme Jackson. As we stood in the afternoon light, wine glasses in hand, I described my concerns about how we filter our perceptions and asked if he were aware of the problem.

"Sure," he said (and I'm paraphrasing). "In neuroscience, we call these filters 'frames.' They are well documented. People create them right up until they are about 37 years old, and then they stop. We live with those frames for the rest of our lives."

Wow. This explained almost everything about the gap between the objective world – a world that could be scientifically proven to exist – and the worlds that we all live in day to day.

Making Frames

Imagine a baby's brain. It's Day One, and this biocomputer doesn't know what a language is, what a room is, what anything is.

After its eyes are working properly, and it's learned to take in sight and make sense of those signals, it sees a leaf. But since it doesn't know what a leaf is, it looks at every part of that leaf: all of the edges, the stem, the veins, the colors, the shape, the top, the bottom, how it flexes in the wind.

The next time it sees a leaf, it does the same thing, all over again.

Now imagine how much of this biocomputer's storage and processing power is being used during this intensive focus on each leaf. What happens next? The biocomputer classifies what it has learned, based on patterns and tagged with the word "leaf." The next time it sees a leaf, or a few leaves, it no longer focuses on so much detail; it's just another leaf. A few years later, riding in a car on the highway past a forest of leaves, that same biocomputer doesn't even pause; it just notes "Forest," knowing that it contains millions of leaves.

It no longer sees the leaves.

This saves a lot of computing space in the brain.

But there's a downside: it no longer sees the world clearly, in detail. Rather, it sees the world through self-imposed filters. Most of us don't see the world clearly at all; rather, we see a filtered abstract of the world.

In one way, this is a normal, highly evolved and advanced state of brain function: it's efficient. But in another sense, the baby's biocomputer was better at seeing the world than the adult's, because it noticed everything.

In order to clearly see the patterns, we have to first be able to see the world in detail. And the only way for an adult to see it is to learn to drop those frames, to let those filters fall away.

Standing on the lawn with Graeme, I realized that this was the key to learning how to see the objective world – the world that, if we dropped our frames, we could all agree on.

The reason to make this effort was clear to me then: that's how you find the basic patterns that lead to discovery and understanding of the real world. Recognizing these patterns, and resolving their meaning, is the key to understanding – literally – everything. Graeme had just given me a crucial clue in making this happen.

Getting the Right Ideas

The world is a confusing, complex place, a tumultuous mix of everything interacting with everything else. Add in the question of any individual's personal observational abilities, along with the intentional efforts of many to obscure what is true and real – and the task of seeing the world clearly seems almost impossible.

But learning to see the world is not impossible, and the rewards are terrific.

When he was 16, Albert Einstein asked himself what he would see, were he able to ride along a beam of light, at the speed of light. How did he come to this question? Did he know that by asking it he would become the most famous scientist in history?

When Winston Churchill finally gained the reins of power in World War II Britain, he quickly realized that the British forces would be unable to beat the Germans "in a fair fight." His decision to postpone that fair fight, while using this time to bring in America, was the result of a key insight that helped Britain win the war.

Today, given the cacophony of mass media and the near-infinite number of accessible ideas and intellectual inputs, there's a temptation to lapse into a belief that everything is relative, that all ideas are equally valuable.

But all ideas are not equal; some are blatantly wrong, and have a breathtaking ability to cause damage, while others are only partly right, and are therefore difficult or even dangerous to use.

And some ideas are provably right. Einstein was right about light's pivotal role in the physical universe. Churchill was right about military strategy. Let's be clear about this: many of their colleagues had the wrong ideas, at exactly the same moment in history.

If some ideas are right, and others are disastrously wrong, it isn't hard to see that most people would prefer having access to the right ideas, and to having the ability to discern the difference.

Einstein's right idea led to a revolution in understanding the physical world, and then to creating the atom bomb, and winning the Pacific War. Churchill's strategy led to saving Britain and Western Europe from Nazi domination, and winning the War in Europe.

Whether it's a battle, our current struggle for planetary survival, or finding a cure for cancer, it's clear that right ideas matter; they matter greatly.

The right ideas are those that emerge directly from the world around us, so it's not surprising that getting these ideas requires seeing that world clearly.

What was less obvious to me, at that stage, was that seeing clearly is just the first step to being able to accurately predict the future.

Chapter 3

Predicting the Future

By the time you've finished this book, you may not yet be an expert at predicting the future, but you will have a better understanding of how to recognize patterns, which will help you see beyond the present.

Because it had always been my plan to become a scientist, when making predictions professionally turned out to be my calling, I set up a company – the Strategic News Service – based on predicting events in technology, at the confluence of computing and communications. I delivered those predictions by (initially free) email to the smartest global leaders in technology and finance I could find. (This later evolved into the subscription-based *SNS Global Report on Technology and the Economy.*)

Now *that* was an intellectual challenge.

From the start, it was clear that I'd need to grade my predictions in public, year by year.

It's hard to describe the fear and excitement I had in those early days when clicking the Send button, knowing that any and all mistakes would draw near-instantaneous response from an online audience that included Steve Jobs, Bill Gates, Michael Dell, and Elon Musk, all of whom were reading those predictions, or "calls."

This process has now been repeated most weeks of the year since 1995. Of course, I've made plenty of wrong predictions. But I learn lessons from those mistakes, and it's these lessons that help keep my accuracy rate high. Here's a really important, if obvious, rule: Be certain before you publish. And it isn't cheating. It's an important way of sifting through calls that might go wrong.

All of the assists and influences I described in Chapter 1 have helped me to become the most accurate predictions expert in these fields today, in terms of important calls and graded metrics. But before we get into the specifics of pattern recognition and my prediction successes, let's define "predictions."

What Are (and What Are Not) Predictions?

A prediction – or "call" – *is* specific. It describes a certain event, or numbers, and usually a time frame (often the most difficult part). What a prediction is *not* is some vague feeling that things will go right or wrong. "The economy will crash someday" is not a prediction. A prediction is not a hunch or a guess; there should be strong reasoning behind it.

Today, often what people describe as predictions are really *projections* (fuzzy forecasts) made by those who look at the past through "rear view mirrors" and then add some correcting up or down.

I call that *guessing*, and it's almost certain to be wrong. Here's an example: Whenever someone shows a chart of anything in the future using a straight line, it's a cue to object. With regard to the future, the one thing we can be certain about is that there are almost no straight lines.

"Typical" predictions in the business world look like the line graphs below, with things moving directly upward in a straight line, regardless of global GDP problems, corporate earnings declines, stock market crashes, and the like:

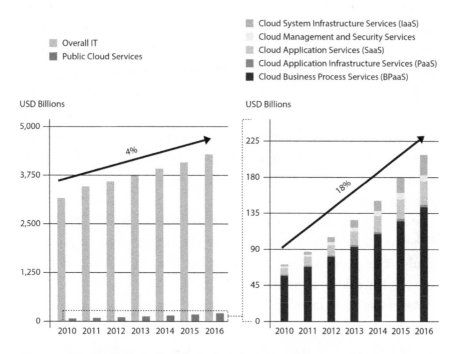

Figure 3-1. Example of a "typical" prediction in the business world.

I don't include this because the numbers themselves are necessarily wrong (although any "straight-line" prediction is likely to be), but because the thinking is wrong. The future almost never unfolds in a straight line.

By contrast, we can look at the Oil Price Collapse of 2014/2015. As mentioned in the Introduction, I seem to have been the only person to publicly make this call (see Chapter 17 for details). The price of oil, with its relatively straight-lined history, suddenly left the norm and dropped by one-half almost overnight. That's how the real world behaves: straight lines are the exception.

In addition to the fuzzy logic of projections, you may also fall short by seeing – and therefore, predicting – part of something, without getting the whole picture. Predicting that a room that's been getting hotter will continue to get hotter might be accurate, but it's a subset of predicting that the building will burn to the ground.

Thousands of people – including Pope Benedict XVI, who now refers to one of his 1985 speeches – have claimed to have "predicted" the 2007/2008 Global Financial Collapse. Most knew that real-estate values just couldn't keep going up. Some knew that the banks seemed to be lending without any controls. Both observations were correct.

But whether looking at national real estate or at Wall Street misbehavior, these people were missing the bigger picture. The room couldn't keep getting hotter forever, but the real problem was that the whole world was about to catch fire.

As stated in a later review by the *Financial Times*, the editors found only three people who publicly and accurately predicted the crash. (I don't think they were counting me, so the number may have been larger.) None were trained economists, and, more important, all three had been watching flows of one kind or another, and were therefore able to see what was behind the real-estate and other valuation bubbles. Those who said they knew price jumps couldn't last forever – well, they were right, too, but that isn't specific enough to be a prediction. Perhaps more to the point, the real-estate market was just a sliver of the global economy.

My chosen task has been to predict large, unforeseen, strategic events across a wide range of territories. It turns out you must look at many different types of patterns even to predict just the technology-related outcomes that readers of our *Global Report* first cared most about. From the personality patterns of a tech CEO to the buying patterns of teens or the voting patterns of the Japanese public, all contribute to outcomes, and so all need to be on my radar.

While it is true that expanding your areas of pattern searching improves prediction accuracy in your fields of knowledge, it has a secondary, fascinating effect: it increases your ability to make accurate predictions in unexpected fields.

The result has found me writing, for example, about Steve Jobs' return to Apple, likely before Steve himself knew he would return; and predicting that China would fire live missiles toward Taiwan just days before it happened.

There are people today who call such important, unexpected events "black swans" because they didn't see them coming. But I just call them "the future." The future is full of discontinuous trends and events.

For prediction experts, there are no black swans – only the ugly ducklings of missed calls.

Patterns Made, Patterns Broken

The discoveries and successful predictions described in this book all happened through two basic steps: learning to see patterns more clearly and understanding what they mean – *pattern resolution*. Pattern resolution can be divided into two major groups: patterns made and patterns broken.

We're all familiar with the idea of "patterns made": it just describes things or events that become recognizable as patterns because they keep doing what they're doing. From musical scales to weather patterns to the personalities of CEOs, once we see clearly what the patterns are, our daily prediction rate of what will happen next improves.

Another way to say this is that "patterns made" are most useful in stable systems. If this were all there were to predicting, you could just improve your ability to see patterns. The rest would be easy. But since the future is made of change, this isn't enough; you need to be looking for "patterns broken." Everyone is familiar with those small news stories at the back of newspapers that begin with words such as "For the first time on record, temperatures rose above . . . " – or "Contrary to expectations [something in the markets] went up, after going down on all past similar occasions."

These are signs of patterns broken, and finding them is like finding diamonds among the glitter of a sandy beach. They are the first signs of dramatic future change, and, if we notice them, give them enough attention, and properly credit them, they will lead us to making accurate predictions that will be as surprising as they are useful.

Xi Jinping broke a long-standing pattern by making his first speech as president of China to a military audience; past leaders had chosen to give their inaugural talks to civilian groups. (A related pattern breaker was that the majority of the newly elected Chinese Politburo Standing Committee had strong military attachments, even as the size of the committee was dropped from nine to seven, giving the military control of China.) Around that time, I had dinner with a China-expert friend, an American who had spent most of his life there and who's been friends with every Chinese leader starting with Mao himself. I said I thought Xi would be driven by the military in using his new powers, but he assured me this would not be the case. "I know his family," my friend said. "He'll be fine."

I soon made my own prediction in print, and it didn't take long before the truth was out.

Since then, Chinese Navy boats have collided with US Navy boats in hair-raising encounters, with more of the same happening often with our air forces. China has announced an unheard-of Air Defense Zone to the north, another military provocation which represents a sudden shift in Chinese policy and a direct threat to Taiwanese sovereignty.

More dramatically, virtually all of the South China Sea island military conflicts and reclamation have happened under Xi, in a breathtaking expansion of economic claims underlined by military force that few saw coming. At least seven new islands are being built out on undersea reefs, and airstrips and barracks designed for military use have been created at breakneck speed.

The patterns broken had told the story.

Not long ago, I was asked to give a keynote talk to the highly secretive National Geospatial-Intelligence Agency (NGA), at its annual Global Research and Development (GRAND) meeting. (The NGA building is said to be the second-largest in the DC area, right after the Pentagon, yet few know of the NGA's existence.) The people of the NGA are almost certainly the world's best experts at "constrained pattern recognition" – that is, seeing patterns in a well-defined environment. Imagine, for example, assessing battlefield damage or looking for submarines.

For my talk, I had been asked to address the use of pattern recognition in an unconstrained environment. Although I can't share the contents of that talk, I am allowed to share an interview I did with the NGA's radio crew afterward, including a discussion of "patterns made and broken," which you'll find here: https://soundcloud.com/nga_geoint/geointeresting.

The Science of Prediction Success: What's Your Number?

You may not know what your accuracy number is, but we all have one, from stock pickers to weather forecasters to people just casually interested in the future. That number is the ratio of number of accurate predictions made to total number of predictions.

So, what is your number? It's possible that you aren't any good at predicting. Most people aren't, probably because they have never trained themselves to do it.

How hard is it to get a good predictions number? Don't assume that the default condition is 50/50, or 50% correct predictions. Daily life has different odds than a coin toss.

Most people think predicting accurately is impossible, and they're nearly right: attaining a good number is quite difficult. That's why meteorologists – perhaps the most public of professionals in the predictions world – almost *never* track their success rates in public. Some Wall Street analysts are famous for specific good calls, but, having run a hedge fund, I can testify that this is actually less about predicting and much more about a delicate dance between the CEO, with her pre-announcements and earnings guidance, and the analyst, with his reports, bound in an unspoken deal.

Think of it this way: you're going to make a prediction about something of your choosing. There are a very small number of correct predictions possible, and an infinite number of ways to get it wrong. The default condition becomes zero. Getting 0% of predictions right is probably normal, which is likely why making accurate predictions is considered almost impossible. When someone tells you that they cannot predict the future, it pays to believe them – because it's hard, and they probably can't.

Imagine, however, that you've spent some time working on this. Perhaps you've read this book and started noticing more patterns around you, and you've been training yourself to see these and make good predictions. A year goes by, and pretty soon you're getting one out of 10 right. In that case, you should congratulate yourself: you're better at this than almost anyone else on the planet. Your number is 10% and growing.

What will matter much more than your number, of course, is that you will then be living proof of something that very few people in the world know: it is possible to predict the future. And if you pay even more attention, you'll probably achieve more accuracy. How far you want to take this most useful ability is up to you.

Because I think the science and metrics of predicting are important, I spent the first 18 months of publishing the *SNS Global Report* grading every prediction, once per quarter, until my readers began to revolt. "Enough already," seemed to be their view. They had become believers, and wanted to move along and focus on the work at hand.

After that, I found a new way to present my "grades": every December, I release 10 predictions for the year ahead, at our annual SNS Predictions Dinner in New York. The global press gets a copy of the new and the old predictions, with the latter publicly graded and open for correction by email and on our website. These also go out on the *BBC World News* to some 220 million listeners, who first are treated to the prior year's calls.

What's my number? My current number, based on over 20 years of making predictions, is 94.7%. I'm working on getting it back up to 95, but at this point I'm not sure it's ever going to happen.

Part 2

Using Patterns to Predict the Future

Chapter 4

From Pattern Recognition to Pattern Discoveries: What's Missing in the Scientific Method

Not long after I realized that I wasn't going to become a scientist – when I was in my early 20s, soon after leaving a PhD program – I decided to follow up on a physics problem that had occurred to me during a professor's lecture at Stanford In 1969.

The question was this: How can a wave of light go to maximum energy, then to zero, then back to maximum, while traveling through empty space? The answer: It can't. But that's exactly what the professor (and the rest of the world of physics at the time) was proposing. There are just a few laws in physics that nobody – and I mean no one, ever – gets to violate. The first of these is the law of conservation of energy, which basically states that energy can't be created or destroyed; and, in a closed system, it remains constant.

In other words, it doesn't go to maximum, then to zero, then back to maximum.

It did not occur to me at the time that this question would lead me to tackle the most difficult problem in science, which is the subject of the next chapter, on Resonance Theory.

At the time I started working on this problem, I had just finished creating The Whale Museum, the world's first research-based whale museum, in Friday Harbor, Washington. Suddenly I found myself out of a job. I was living in an old rented house on a harbor, built by a shipwright, with a long dark wooden dining table facing the seaside window. What better place to solve a fascinating problem?

Asking the Right Question

If the question was, Where does the wave's energy go when it appears to go to zero? the answer had to be that it was stored in space itself. Of course, most physicists of the time had convinced themselves that this was not a problem – that various forms of mathematics and field expressions made it a non-issue. I just wasn't convinced of that; I thought they were fooling themselves.

Since light is the result of electric and magnetic forces interacting, I realized that in order to succeed in this hunt, I'd need to understand these forces much better. I'd also need to do a huge amount of reading to get up to speed with what was then known in physics regarding light and empty space. I pulled out my not-yet-old physics texts, in addition to collecting a large pile of other texts and articles on this and related subjects. And then a second major question occurred to me, based on an emerging pattern.

I found myself quickly listing laws for all kinds of force, from gravitation to electric – perhaps 13 in all – and they all had a similar mathematical structure. How could that be?

Why were all of these force laws expressed in the same form?

Despite what you might think goes on in a university setting, in my experience you don't really get a chance to ask fundamental questions, such as "What is a force?" or "Why are so many forces expressed in a single type of equation?"

I'd done enough reading to know what the reigning physicists thought about unifying force laws as they worked toward building what they called the Standard Model – the group effort to create a Theory of Everything, which would unify all of physics.

But I didn't trust the version of physics I'd been taught at Stanford. It wasn't that I thought the leading scientists were wrong, so much as I didn't think they were right. Science in general had lost its way, to my view. I'd seen enough of it, as an undergraduate and then during my stints as a grad student, to know that it was badly broken.

There are two really great examples I like to use to explain how dysfunctional the science world is today.

First, there's the Scientific Method – the system all scientists have used, since science began. Most of us are taught this stuff in grade school, and it goes something like this: Take an idea (a hypothesis), test it with an experiment, analyze the results, and then, modifying that idea, do it again.

This is how all scientific progress is made. Or so our teachers tell us.

But it turns out they've forgotten to teach the most important part. Where and how are we to get ideas? It's even worse than that: history clearly shows us that the quality of the initial question is the greatest contributor to whether the result is trivial or wonderfully productive.

Why is there no focus on getting the right idea? This isn't just important – it's everything.

When you study the great breakthroughs in science, you see that they usually come to an individual in a windfall moment after he'd been mentally chewing away at a problem; they almost never arrive *during* that intense process. Rather, it's in a dream (Kekulé), or when stepping off a tram (Descartes), or while daydreaming (Newton). The brain does its best work if you give it exhaustive preparation and then let it "step away," free-associating in its search for solutions.

But these days, for a variety of social, publication, academic, and funding reasons, coming up with radical new ideas tends to be a career-ending move. The most welcoming ideas today are those that are non-threatening to your peers and non-disruptive to the larger, agreed-upon path of the crowd. They should always be submitted for publication through a known university lab, and they should include many known names as authors, the first being the most senior and "safest."

That may be a great way to make Volkswagens, but it wouldn't work for Ferraris.

The result, particularly in physics, has been a creeping incrementalism, and a replacement of "Getting the Right Idea" as the question driving the scientific method with "Getting an Idea We Can All Agree Upon."

I can illustrate the second example of how broken science is by asking and answering just one question: What would happen to Einstein if he were starting his career today?

In 1905, what we now call the "wonder year" of physics, Albert Einstein was an examiner in the Berne patent office. During that year, he finished his PhD. Translation: He was a nobody.

But in 1905, he published four papers in the *Annalen der Physik*,[1] then the world's leading physics journal. These papers created the foundation for Quantum Mechanics and Special Relativity – the two mainstreams of physics – which stand tall, and still separate, today. Together, these papers described the photoelectric effect, quantumization, Brownian motion and statistical mechanics, Special Relativity, and mass-energy equivalence.

So, here's the problem: there's no way that any of these, much less all four, would have been published today if submitted within today's requirements. Each was radical and controversial, submitted under

---

[1] Albert Einstein, the "Annus Mirabilis" papers on photoelectric effect, Brownian motion, special theory of relativity, and mass-energy equivalence, *Annalen der Physik*, 1905.

Einstein's name only, with no co-authors or university to stand or hide behind and no big names at the top of the papers.

And that's what's wrong with science, and particularly with physics, today.

Because I didn't trust this process, I didn't trust the answers it generated. And because I didn't trust the answers, I felt that I had to go back to basics and start building my own picture of how the world really worked, using patterns as my primary guide.

Unifying 13 Force Laws (with a Commodore 64)

In order to see things more clearly, I thought it made sense to get my tools out of the books and into the open, onto a large surface where I could quickly see and compare the many equations of basic physics and their resulting patterns.

My attack plan was simple: buy a box of colored pens and a roll of butcher paper. By sliding the paper back and forth across the dining-room tabletop as needed, and using colors to represent the various fields of physics and their force laws, I could see perhaps two full tabletops' worth of information. In real terms, I was able to look at something like 48 square feet of color-coded equations – with notes and arrows connecting them – instead of the usual book pages. If helping the brain find patterns was the right path, this was a huge leap forward.

It didn't take long to get about 13 different fields of physics down on paper, with the force laws for each. After a bit of work, I was able to generalize these laws into a single equation with very simple rules. By then I had been spending weeks alone at this table, while family meals were relegated to the living room; and I had no idea whether what I'd found was important.

On the one hand, I'd made what seemed like a pretty amazing

discovery (rolling 13 forces into one), but I needed to check my growing theory with someone in the field who was up-to-date on modern physics, and who would also have a mind open to seeing new things. Almost magically, the chance presented itself.

Going to the Masters

Later, as this kind of experience became more common, I gave a name to this "checking in" with brilliant people – experts in their field – to make sure I was on track: I call it "Going to the Masters." I didn't know it at the time, but I was developing a new (to me, at least) way of learning about the world: first, drop your frames; second, seek patterns; third, integrate the patterns into a new understanding, almost a metapattern; and finally, Go to the Masters – check out your results with the most brilliant people available.

So it was that one afternoon I was sitting on a porch at sunset with a professor friend when he mentioned knowing Dr. William Bender, then an emeritus professor of physics at Western Washington University. He was kind enough to soon introduce us, and Bill was generous enough with his time to agree to see an unknown amateur physicist wannabe.

From then on, every two weeks or so I'd fly to Bellingham, bringing the derivations for that session's field of physics and demonstrating its connection to my generalized equation. Bill would sit at the back of the room, making comments. In each case, he agreed that I had succeeded.

It's hard to describe how exhilarating it was to have found something new in physics, with a radically different point of view, and to have done it in this way.

In order to demonstrate this new unification path, I decided to try a kind of parlor trick: I had just purchased a shiny new Commodore 64 computer, which was linked up to my color TV. In no time, I had written a program that used the single equation at its core to answer questions and solve problems, with 13 different user interfaces, depending on the user's preferred field of physics.

It was a way of using software to prove the unification of these force laws. The proof was simple: it worked.

You could tell the computer what you were interested in – say, gravitational force, or Special Relativity effects – and it would ask you about rest masses, or relative velocity, or electric force; and it would ask you about charges, and so on. Then it would calculate the resulting force, no matter the area of interest.

I was ready to turn back to my original question: What happens to the "missing energy" when light moves through empty space?[2] What I wasn't ready for: creating the next Theory of Everything.

---

[2] Mark R. Anderson, "Resonance Theory," *SNS Special Report*, 2011, Fig. 1, http://www.stratnews.com/resonance/.

Chapter 5

Creating Resonance Theory and Finding Einstein's Biggest (Real) Mistake

If you like puzzles, this should interest you; it is the most difficult puzzle in the world. I couldn't resist trying out what I'd learned about patterns to break it wide open.

Physicists aren't alone in their almost religious belief that, at the very core of the universe, all is one. In physics, the search for a Theory of Everything is a search to find a single law that unifies all of the forces, and a single explanation for all particles and their behaviors.

This really is the greatest puzzle of all time – at least in the objective world. I didn't see any particular reason it wouldn't succumb to my butcher-paper approach. During those two years, I read everything I could find on the subject, in every case looking for patterns that would unveil a deeper truth or symmetry in this hunt for a great unifying law.

In all of this work, I kept light – electromagnetic radiation – at the center of my pattern search. While it seemed that, to many researchers, photons (light as a particle) were just one more piece of the particle zoo, I saw it very differently. Light's constant speed, and its role in very important energy equations, gave it a central role that fit in no other patterns. Light was different, and, for me, became the central character in the story of how the world – and (otherwise) empty space – worked.

I was already starting to resist the common term "empty space" in relation to light, because I knew it had electrical and magnetic properties and that it could store energy. With all that going on, it obviously was not the "void" that classical physics proposed. And while many quantum physicists agreed that there was something that allowed for a "quantum foam" to occur in space, they didn't go any further in describing it; it was more like a "cheat," something allowed inside certain tiny boundaries too small to be seen, and therefore was OK.

I don't like cheats, or tricks, even when I understand them.

The hunt progressed in several phases. Four, to be exact.

Enter Resonance Theory

First, I'd shown a new way to represent the major forces.

Second, I'd proven the necessity of empty space not being empty, but rather being capable of energy storage. I may not have known all that it *was* – but whatever it was, it wasn't empty; it had real physical characteristics, which could be measured to many decimal places.

Third, it was clear that space therefore could resonate, given an "injection" of energy. My guess was that the result was what we call particles, or light waves. For this reason, because all things were created out of empty space resonating, I decided to call my findings Resonance Theory.

I also went off on many tangents. I spent a lot of time thinking about particles versus waves, in order to understand how (otherwise) empty space worked. In the end, I landed on this stumper question: What is a wave? Like 16-year-old Einstein, I wanted to know: What would we see if we traveled alongside a light wave at the speed of light?

One thing is certain: it wouldn't look like a wave. It might not look like a particle, either.

Spoiler alert: I haven't solved this problem yet.

I looked at how light waves are formed as they come off an antenna, and this was incredibly helpful. In fact, it led me to the suspicion that the ultimate mathematics for describing resonant events in (otherwise empty) space had a strong resemblance to the creations of Sir Roger Penrose, perhaps the most brilliant mathematician alive, who called them "spinors" and "twistors."

I turned back to the "missing energy" problem in the first question – How could it be missing? – and calculated, in quantity and geometry, exactly how space must be storing that energy. For lack of a better idea, I proposed this new wave as a "mass wave." This was a reach, but since all energy is convertible to mass, I figured I could work with that.

It seemed to me that Einstein's proof of space and time curving in the presence of mass was exactly what was happening inside each wavelength of light.

Cardboard Geometry

I made some other discoveries, which are less about Resonance Theory than about finding other patterns, both mathematical and geometric – in our world, in physics.

In one case, I was able to create a geometry that could be turned into a small cardboard tool that produced all of the equations of Special Relativity. It was so simple that I was able to win a bet with the local science teacher: that I could teach Special Relativity to an eighth-grade class in our town in 10 minutes, followed by a short quiz – which everyone passed.

This led to a very deep question. Velocity in this tool was expressed not as feet per second, for example, but as an angle. As far as I could tell, this appeared to violate all kinds of things in accepted physics. I was going to need some type of verification, if this were true.

Putting It All Together

Fourth, I was finally able to put the pieces together, at least in my own mind.

But before that, I was still struggling to wrap my head around the whole thing. I'd worked on light refraction and reflection, empty space from both quantum and relativity perspectives, symmetry groups, and tensor mathematics. All of it was sitting somewhere in my head, not yet properly ordered, with space and light in the middle.

One night, near the end of all this work, it was time for a break. It was late, and as I walked out into the grass, the full moon was shining down in a path across the harbor waters. The sun, I knew, was creating light waves and sending them out, and the moon was reflecting those waves down to Earth, where the light reflected again on the water and bounced into my eyes.

Space wasn't empty – it was what light was made of – and so were particles. So was the sun, and the moon, and the Earth, and the water on the Earth, and . . . The lightbulb went on.

Everything, all of it, was space resonating and interacting with itself.

That remains the most indescribably exciting intellectual and spiritual moment of my life.

At that point, I also realized there was just one small problem. I had created a lot of very radical proposals. They seemed to work, on paper. But were they true? It was time to go to the masters.

Going to the Masters

To me, "going to the masters" meant making a list of the leading physicists around the world who had done work that I felt, in various ways, was linked to or compatible with Resonance Theory. If they would meet with me, I'd travel to meet with them – and see if we could agree on the part or parts of Resonance Theory that applied to each of them in some new way in their own work.

This list included John Cramer, James Cronin, David Bohm, Roger Penrose, and Richard Feynman. They were among the most highly respected physicists alive, and I felt some anxiety as well as excitement over the idea of trying to show them something new in laws of the world they knew better than anyone.

Master 1: John Cramer

I started with John Cramer, having visited him a few times before, thanks to an introduction by the dean of physics at the University of Washington. John is a brilliant nuclear physicist who is open to new ideas; today he's advanced from being a top professor to professor emeritus, but then he was still relatively young, and in the middle of his career.

I asked him if he knew of anything in physics that would parallel my increasingly strong view that velocity could be treated as an angle rather than as distance over time. Since Einstein had proved theoretically that all velocity is relative, this could pose some real problems among observers, which we both knew.

It only took him a few seconds to respond.

"Sure. There was an experiment just recently which appeared to show that an electron's spin angle increases based on its relative velocity."

What the . . .?! I wrote down the name of the effect, thanked him, and left, in a daze.

Electrons, like many other particles, have a "spin angle," which one might (improperly) envision as though something were spinning in an orbit around the electron. If this orbit is "straight up" when at rest, John was telling me, then as its relative motion increases, the angle increases at the same time.

Although this didn't bear directly on Resonance Theory, it did have immediate consequences for some of the other work I'd done, which suddenly seemed to have moved from a crazy "what-if" geometrical view to something much more serious.

Master 2: James Cronin

Next up was Nobel-winning particle physicist James Cronin, who was working at the University of Chicago, where he was professor emeritus of astronomy and physics. Cronin's primary work, with his colleague Val Logsdon Fitch, was to show something called "charge parity (CP) violation." In plain English, this means that things don't work the same way going forward in time as going backward. This blew everyone's mind.

But the reason I wanted to talk with him was that he had a deep understanding of "Lamb shift," which has to do with how atoms are structured, the energy state of electrons around those atoms, and how space itself affects (and changes) both.

If Resonance Theory were correct, then you could think of an atom as a kind of building made out of space itself. Each particle in the atom would be a small standing wave made of space, and you could – at least theoretically – build larger structures by literally "piling" these resonating waves on top of one another.

In other words, there would be a kind of physical fit to these building blocks, these resonances that everyone was calling protons, and electrons, and neutrons. I knew almost nothing beyond Physics 101 about Cronin's field, but I thought he might sense the rightness-or-wrongness of my concept and give me some feedback.

I went to see him early in the afternoon, navigating several long hallways to get to his (rather small) office. He was very kind, but also in a bit of a hurry. I got right down to business, describing the idea of space itself as the material from which particles are made, space interacting with itself as the way forces are expressed, the characteristics of space itself describing what leads to the family of long-lived particles such as electrons, and so on.

He listened. I think he might have asked one question.

"Does this make sense to you?" I asked. "Do you think this could be how atoms are structured?"

He was not excited; I could tell that right away. He even seemed a bit testy. Maybe he was just in a hurry to get somewhere else.

"It's possible."

I need to explain something now to the nonphysicists in the crowd: In the world of physics theory, all theories are true unless proven wrong. This sounds funny, but it comes from long experience. The purpose of feedback on a theory is to prove it wrong, which happens just about all of the time.

So, for James Cronin to say what he said, at least to my understanding, was a Big Deal.

Then came the hammer.

"Would you mind showing me the mathematics behind your reasoning?"

This was a problem, for two reasons.

First, the theory was still an unpublished secret, and the last thing I wanted to do was risk giving the whole thing away to someone much more powerful in that world than me.

But there was a second, much larger, problem with showing him the math: I couldn't.

Sure, I had done many years of math at Stanford, but this was a level of the game that I was completely unprepared for. And it shows up one of the problems in making discoveries by using patterns: you might be right, but you will not have gone through the same doors and windows as everyone else in the room.

When they start asking you to speak their language, in their context – it's very difficult.

I froze. And then I bolted. Part of this was just nerves, but the result was, I thanked him for his time and was out of there like a shot.

But not before I'd acquired a whole new understanding of How to Build Atoms 101.

Master 3: David Bohm

Next up was David Bohm, an incredible scientist who had been Einstein's friend and colleague. He had discovered some really amazing physics on his own, and, with his permanent sidekick, B.J. Hiley, had been working for years on unifying relativity and quantum mechanics – the two worlds Einstein had split, in what came to be known as his Biggest Mistake.

Bohm was at Birkbeck College, University of London. At the time of our appointment , his wife was terminally ill and in the hospital. I was afraid he'd need to cancel, but he insisted by phone that we could still meet, so I went to his office on a summer afternoon. The shades were drawn, creating a kind of eerie stillness inside the darkened room. He sat at his desk, B.J. standing quietly nearby.

Here was one of the world's leading physicists, who had published a book titled *Wholeness and the Implicate Order,* and who was therefore totally focused on the prime proposal of Resonance Theory. He might have been the smartest of all those in the competition to unify these two fields, and there were hundreds, if not thousands, of others working on the same problem.

I explained the theory. I touched on Einstein's Biggest Mistake. I explained why the speed of light (C) is not just measured in meters per second, but also in the ratio of electrical and magnetic properties of space, one of the real clues in my work on this problem. How could a velocity also be an electromagnetic ratio, unless space – and physics – were very different from what we'd all been taught?

Space isn't empty; it has these characteristics, and the laws of physics derive directly from the properties of otherwise-empty space.

Then I stopped, and waited.

Bohm and B.J. asked me a series of questions, all of which seemed easy to answer; it took less than five minutes.

They were very quiet, both just looking at me, then at each other.

"Could you come back and join us again in the morning?" Bohm asked.

I said I couldn't, because I had an appointment with Roger Penrose at Oxford.

We talked a little longer, I thanked him for taking time with me when his wife was so ill, and left.

I still remember, as I walked down the hall, thinking: He gets it. He totally gets it. He's asking you to come back. He gets it.

Unfortunately, as fate would have it, I never saw David again.

Master 4: Roger Penrose

By almost all accounts, Roger Penrose was already the best mathematician in the world when I went to visit him on a sunny morning at Oxford University, in 1980. As we walked into his office, he mentioned that he was spending most of his time on quantum chromodynamics, which had become a hot new field.

He was very pleasant, and we got right down to business. I was getting more comfortable explaining the Resonance Theory program to my chosen masters, even if each presentation was geared for the field of the scientist I was visiting at the time.

I told him that I thought his "twistor" mathematics was the closest thing I had seen to something that represented the purest description of the events of energy resonating in (otherwise) empty space. He seemed very interested in this interpretation.

I expected that he was working on an agenda for using twistors broadly in describing particles, and I was heartened that he felt this was congruous with Resonance Theory.

He then asked a single question, with a kind of small smile; it felt a bit like a test, perhaps one he had a personal stake in.

"Does your work suggest that neutrinos do, or do not, have rest mass?"

In 1980, this was a big deal. There was a lot of debate in the scientific world over whether neutrinos could travel at or beyond the speed of light, and whether they had rest mass.

"If they travel at the speed of light, they certainly don't have rest mass," I replied.

He seemed to like this answer, which was classical, but also apparently reassuring on some level. If this was a test, it felt as though, all in all, I had just passed it.

"So what can I do for you?" he asked. I told him I planned to put a paper together and would appreciate any feedback on it prior to publishing.

He said he'd be happy to do so. I thanked him, we exchanged addresses, and I left.

It was, I thought, a great meeting. Twistors were now a top candidate for the mathematics of Resonance Theory, and Penrose himself seemed to agree.

Less than a year later, I sent him the first draft of my paper, showing a dissected light wave with not only electric and magnetic fields, but also the "missing energy" (mass) field as well, all packaged in a physical string made of (otherwise) empty space. In the Acknowledgments section, I thanked him for his input, making it clear that he had no responsibility for the paper's contents, right or wrong.

He didn't write back.

I wrote to him again. No answer. This seemed strange. I assumed there was a problem of some kind.

During this period, and after my paper's first rejection, I discovered that a new theory of everything, called String Theory, had just been published (at the same time as my submission), by Michael Green; it proposed vibrating strings in a number of dimensions as the answer to the Theory of Everything search.

While Resonance Theory was different, it did use string mathematics to describe a vibrating string, which was the reason it was rejected by *Physical Review*.

Not long afterward, in the mid-'80s, I saw Penrose again, at the University of Washington; he said he'd not seen the paper, but if I would fax it to him right now, he'd take a look. I did. No response.

Only then did I find out that he was apparently in some kind of intellectual combat with the string theorists – no doubt hoping that twistors would prevail.

Aha.

And here is the funniest part of this strange story. In 2003 (23 years later), Edward Witten, the leading string theorist of that era, proposed a way of merging string and twistor mathematics, calling it Twistor String Theory. Suddenly – rumor had it – Roger no longer hated strings.

I have always wondered if he remembered that young amateur, the guy who wrote the first or second string-theory paper, suggesting to him in 1980 that twistors are the answer to the string problem.

No Dice, No Glory, but That's OK

I spent a few years trying to get my paper published, but only in that one publication – the best and hardest to get into – the *Physical Review*. I was being vain: now that the whole world knew about String Theory, I wanted my place in line to be maintained. I didn't want to publish the same paper as the 300th string paper, or whatever it was, rather than the first, or the second.

The well-known physicist and author Fred Alan Wolfe, who was personal friends with the editor of *Physical Review*, offered to help. We spent hours going over my paper to make sure he was comfortable with it, then composing a cover letter asking to keep the same date and serial number of the original submission, and please – please – to publish the original paper.

No dice. The editor refused to answer questions about the science or the dated serial number, and continued to refuse to publish the paper.

Finally, I got tired of this nonsense and published it myself, through the Strategic News Service. I included all of the documentation – complete with the unintelligible replies from the editor – so that others could see how goofy the science publishing business had become.

The good news, as far as I'm concerned, is that since the day I finished writing it, nothing has been discovered to disprove Resonance Theory, and many, many things have now been discovered which support it. To the best of my knowledge, now a quarter of a century later, it is absolutely correct.

What does it tell us?

The laws of physics derive directly from the properties of (otherwise) empty space.

In other words, space is not empty, and physicists had been studying the wrong things – the particles – rather than the stuff of which they are made, which is the stuff of space. This remains as true today as it was when I wrote that first paper.

Perhaps someday I'll have reason to write the other two papers that will wrap it up. In each case, the basic (and radical) pattern discoveries fell out of applying pattern recognition to past mathematics – a rather novel way of doing physics.

Einstein's Biggest Mistake

By the time I wrote the Resonance paper, I'd intensively studied Einstein – his life, his ideas, and his publications. Here I was, trying to tie up all of physics with a nice ribbon, and he – the guy who'd discovered both relativity and quantum mechanics – had failed in his own lifelong attempts to unify them. Why, I wondered, after a century's worth of efforts, had no one been able to do it?

I backtracked the problem to when, as a teenager, Einstein was first looking at light, and at the scientific work of the time. The physics world was embroiled in an argument about space, about light, and about what space was "made of": it was being called the "ether," but no one could properly describe it.

Even though Einstein and others knew that empty space had electric and magnetic characteristics, he just set all that aside in his work – I think for political reasons. Who needed the fight and the political anguish?

I found a quote from Einstein in a later book, *The Evolution of Physics*, which he co-authored with Leopold Infeld:

> All our attempts to make ether real failed. It revealed neither its mechanical construction nor absolute motion. Nothing remained of all the properties of the ether except that for which it was invented, i.e. its ability to transmit electromagnetic waves. Our attempts to discover the properties of the ether led to difficulties and contradictions. After such bad experiences, this is the moment to forget the ether completely and to try never to mention its name. We shall say: our space has the physical property of transmitting waves, and so omit the use of a word we have decided to avoid.

The omission of a word from our vocabulary is, of course, no remedy. Our troubles are indeed much too profound to be solved in this way![1]

If you mention Einstein's Biggest Mistake, most people would undoubtedly assume you're talking about one of the two so-called "mistakes" he discussed publicly: his letter to Franklin D. Roosevelt encouraging the US president to build the atom bomb, and the "cosmological constant" in his General Relativity Theory.

But I was convinced that his biggest mistake was totally different: ignoring the ability of empty space to pass light, through its inherent magnetic and electric characteristics. These were well-described before his day, everyone knew about them, they were enshrined in famous equations about light – but he just threw them in the can, together with the "ether." The result was a century of unresolved physical laws, with the worlds of charge and mass, quantum mechanics and general relativity, never united.

I was so convinced this was the case that I wrote a special SNS publication called "Einstein's Biggest Mistake."[2] Here we go again, I thought, as I put my neck firmly on the public chopping block. Who was I to make such a claim?

A couple years later, Walter Isaacson (president and CEO of the Aspen Institute) had begun research on a biography of Einstein. I talked with him about the project and then sent him a copy of "Einstein's Biggest Mistake" and some related research. A few months later, I saw Walter again in Aspen.

"You were right!" he said. "Did you know that Einstein himself admitted that this was his greatest mistake?"

---

[1] Albert Einstein and Leopold Infeld, *The Evolution of Physics* (New York: Simon & Schuster, 1988).

[2] Mark R. Anderson, "Einstein's Biggest Mistake," *SNS Technology Letter*, June 17, 2003, https://www.stratnews.com/recent/mode/show/issue/2003-06-17/.

I'd had no idea. It seemed beyond the realm of great fortune.

"Yes," he went on. "He admitted it in a speech, which he gave to the faculty and students at Leiden University, in 1920."

Well, *that* worked out.

Here, in that May 5 address, the most famous scientist in world history is reversing course and "eating crow," 15 years after cutting the world of physics in two [emphasis mine]:

> The ether appears indistinguishable in its functions from ordinary matter. Within matter it takes part in the motion of matter and in empty space it has everywhere a velocity; so that the ether has a definitely assigned velocity throughout the whole of space. There is no fundamental difference between Hertz's ether and ponderable matter (which in part subsists in the ether). . . .
>
> **To deny the ether is ultimately to assume that empty space has no physical qualities whatever. The fundamental facts of mechanics do not harmonize with this view.**[3]

Unfortunately, I had to figure this out for myself, since my talk with Walter came a couple decades after Resonance Theory.

By then I'd burned through all our savings, and a good deal of family goodwill, and, as my very patient wife finally put it, it was time to get a real job.

---

[3] From "Ether and the Theory of Relativity," an address by Albert Einstein delivered at the University of Leiden, translated from German to English (London: Methuen & Co. Ltd, 1922).

Chapter 6

Sometimes It Really Is Rocket Science

My friend Elon Musk asked if he could fly up to have lunch together. It didn't seem to faze him a bit that he lived in California and I lived on a small island in Washington. "Of course," I said. "Sure."

That afternoon, over lunch in a waterfront restaurant, he described what he wanted to achieve in solar power and why the technology wasn't quite ready yet. We talked about electric cars and a list of other topics. Then he got to the point of his visit.

"I want to start a rocket company," he said. "I think it can be done for a lot less than it's being done for today, and I think I can do it. Maybe for 10 times less, in cost per pound of payload. Some of my friends think it's a good idea, some think I'm crazy. What do you think?"

We talked about how he could save money on fuel tanks, what the market would be in the future, how hard it might be to break into the bids for these launches – after which it took me about 38 seconds to answer.

My nearly lifelong fascination with rockets – nurtured and indulged by my patient father in the days of my young biocomputer's development – made it easy. "Do I think it's a good idea? Yes – as long as you put me on your advisory board. I think it's a terrific idea!"

Today, Space Exploration Inc. (SpaceX) is arguably the most fascinating company in the world. Not only is it still private, but it's also the first privately held company to do a long list of things, including resupply the International Space Station.

Elon Musk: Master of Pattern Resolution

In addition to being one of the most successful entrepreneurs alive today, Elon is a pretty interesting guy. He has a singular ability to look at the global landscape, see what will be needed in the long term, assess the technologies available to address all of the key issues involved, look at the science involved, sense the market and tech timing in it all, wrap it into a business plan, and make it go.

Pattern recognition and pattern resolution: these two processes are the key to Elon's intellectual success, I think. Seeing the patterns in the objective world and then figuring out what they mean and what to do about them: this is as close to magic as we come in the world of science. And what Elon has achieved with Tesla Motors, his electric-vehicle company; with SpaceX; and with SolarCity, his solar installation company, is nothing short of modern magic.

Over the years he's been creating these companies, Elon has been kind enough to join me onstage at our annual Future in Review (FiRe) conference; he was there for our first year, in 2003, and has been with us seven years all told. We've test-driven and sold Tesla prototypes at FiRe, cheered his first successful launches in live-streaming events, and interviewed his cousin Lyndon Rive, then CEO of SolarCity, his third company at the time.

A few years ago, we decided to give Elon our first FiRe Entrepreneur of the Year award, preceded by an hour-long interview that – for the first time in FiRe history – ran to 90 minutes. At the end of this riveting conversation, I asked him the most difficult, and most important, question I could think of. Here was a person, after all, who was making essentially all of the critical engineering, design, and business decisions for the world's most advanced car and rocket companies.

"Elon, please explain something to me. You're both the CEO and the chief technology officer of SpaceX. You have no real training in aeronautics. Let's say two engineers, each of whom has spent a whole career in the field, come to you with a disagreement: one wants this valve, and one believes in the other valve. You have to make the decision, and clearly, you make the right one. How do you do that?"

Even 10 seconds of silence on a live stage is a very long time, and I think I sat there, waiting for Elon's response, for most of a minute. (You can watch the video of this event.[1]) Finally, I accepted that he wasn't going to answer a question that clearly had only one answer.

"OK, I'll answer for you. You're just that smart. You are smart on a level that most people probably don't even understand."

Elon, being a gentleman, just smiled and accepted the award.

But here's my real point: Elon isn't just smart – he's a master at pattern resolution. Perhaps better than anyone I know, he has evolved the ability to look at patterns all around the world, resolve them into a few critical categories that need to be addressed, and provide the solutions. He can look at transportation patterns and pick the electric-car solution, and then look at all of the patterns around it and select batteries and charging stations as the critical issues. He can look at all of the patterns around lithium batteries and pick the one or two things (safety, temperature regulation) that are most critical for commercial success, and resolve solutions for these problems.

And when two engineers at SpaceX bring him two different, highly specialized valves with competing designs, he can recall everything

---

[1] "Blast Off! From Launching Private Rockets to the Next Electric Cars," video of Mark Anderson and Elon Musk at FiRe 2009 conference, https://www.youtube.com/watch?v=XdJZVUMRoTg&feature=youtu.be.

he's read about valves, remember the patterns shared by the most successful designs, and pick the right one.

Now *that's* rocket science.

How an Eight-Year-Old Used Pattern Recognition to Build a Better Rocket

When I was a kid, my father used to get *Aviation Week*, which was chock-full of jet fighters and rockets. And I'd read every issue. I loved it; I loved everything about planes and rockets.

I built models of all of the US rockets of the day. And while each was different – some had three stages, some two, and one even had five – they all shared this pattern: there were several stages on top of one another, each with its own fuel tank, each sitting on top of an engine with thrust nozzles underneath. When you looked at them from the side, they looked skinny and tall. How many more stages could be added? This actually seemed to be the operative problem, given the pattern in their designs.

One day I realized that this design pattern was completely wrong. I could tell that the rocket scientists were running out of ideas, stacking more and more stages in search of more powerful results, and clearly reaching the point at which this pattern would break. You can't put 17 stages on top of one another.

Instead of each stage carrying all of the inert fuel of all the other stages above it, wouldn't it be much more efficient to have multiple stages gathered at the bottom, and burn the fuel as fast as possible?

It suddenly seemed almost as though the real job of a rocket is to get rid of fuel – to get rid of weight as low as possible in the "gravity well."

I told my father the idea. A mechanical engineer, he suggested I write to Dr. Werner von Braun, the famous German scientist then running the post-WWII US rocket program. So I did.

A few weeks later, I got my letter back, plus a box of press materials and photos of rockets. There was no sign of von Braun ever having seen the letter, nor was there any change in how America made its rockets.

That was in 1959. In 1966, at the Paris Air Show, Russia revealed its much-celebrated Vostok rocket – with all of the engines clustered at the bottom. *Time* magazine ran a story saying the CIA and NASA had thought Russia had been using a top-secret new monster engine design, based on radar tracking of its launches. The top US Pentagon brass were apparently relieved that the Vostok was instead "just" a cluster of normal engines.

Today, literally every large rocket in the world is built this way, from the European Arianespace to the SpaceX Falcon 9.

When you see a pattern that you know has to break, you're already halfway to finding a resolution, and, often, the ultimate solution to the larger problem.

In this case, after 50 years and way too many calculus courses, I can explain why a higher burn rate and faster fuel weight-reduction is the right solution set for getting rockets up through the gravity well at the lowest cost. But I certainly had no access to those ideas when I was eight.

That year, I also designed an atomic-scale inertial guidance system, which, as far as I can tell, no one else has discovered. But that's another story.

Chapter 7

Breaking the Savings and Loan Scandal

Having no experience at newspapers or with investigative journalism didn't seem like a large hurdle when, looking for any kind of employment in my small island town, my friend Brad needed a vacation replacement at the local paper. He'd be gone for a couple of weeks, and, after all, how much is there to report in a place with more churches than banks?

"What do you think you'll write about?" Brad asked me on his way out of town.

I had no idea how to answer. How do you write a newspaper story about fishing, or logging, or teens falling in love?

"Ben Doerksen," I told him. Ben was a commercial developer who, the week before, had vanished in the middle of the night (which is hard to do on a ferry-served island), leaving the town's first shopping center half-finished. Not a big story, but maybe more thought-provoking than local football scores.

Brad seemed satisfied, and that was that: suddenly I was a real journalist, with a real paper, with no idea how to do whatever came next.

The rumor was that Ben had taken a pile of cash on his way out of town. He'd also left a long line of angry subcontractors holding the bag, unpaid for all of their most recent work. I set out to get the story.

A Double Mystery

In the next few weeks, I learned a lot about Ben and even more about the broken project. Ben had apparently had problems before, including reports of strange financial doings with one or more nursing homes in Oregon. Described as a "Portland business man" in one account, he had been involved in, and was then bought out of, a company through which he personally imported "carpets, and a large supply of Mao coats," according to the *Eugene Register-Guard*.

I was starting to get the picture.

But people in our town seemed to have liked Ben, at least before he left – although much later I heard other stories that were less complimentary.

Ben gave money to charities, helped out with sports-team funding, joined the local service clubs, gave talks about doing good. He went to church and seemed to know everybody in town. When he pitched the construction of a shopping center, local officials cleared the permits.

Why, I wondered, would someone leave in the middle of a project like this? The place was hardly half-done: almost none of it was finished out, partially built stores were empty, and there was over a score of subcontractors waiting to get paid for work completed.

It didn't make sense. Why not finish and make money? Why run away and stiff your partners? Why ruin your own reputation? And how much money was involved? Was it enough to be a motive?

I was starting to think I'd picked a rat-hole for a story.

A rumor went around about Ben being seen at a gas station on the mainland – maybe someone saw him in Portland, or Northern California. What I didn't know then was that Ben would never be found again. There would be no satisfying story end where the crook breaks down and tells all.

I spent a lot of time with Ben's foreman on the project, who was then in the process of losing everything. He was understandably bitter – so much so that I had to carefully check all of the things he said about Doerksen. But two things were clear: he thought Ben was a crook, and not just some wayward developer; and there was "more to the story." I had the impression that he was waiting for the right moment to spill the beans on what had really happened.

Despite my efforts to learn more from him, that moment never came – not then, not later.

I had run out of leads. Certainly, there was nothing that would indicate this would become one of the largest stories in American financial history and would lead to a death threat before it was finished.

Patterns Emerge

Not only was I not a journalist, but with no background in commercial development, I had a limited number of tools to fall back on. But patterns were starting to crop up that were, well, interesting.

For one, there was a local official we'll call "Barney," the kind of guy who wore white shoes and a white belt in a town where everyone else wore work boots. Wherever I turned, there he was, in name or in person.

And there was a bank, Queen City Savings and Loan – not part of Ben's development, but sitting right in front of it. It was the bank Ben used. At the time, it was the biggest bank in town, a branch of a larger bank company with outlets in Seattle and Texas.

How did Ben get any money out of a half-finished project? I talked to the local bank officers, who said something very interesting: I'd have to talk with Barney, since, as a representative of the bank in this matter, he was technically in charge of approving any fund disbursements.

I went to see Barney – whom I knew, in the same way you know everyone in a small town – and he invited me into his office. I explained the question, and he cheerfully went in search of his last signoff sheet on the project, which he handed to me a couple minutes later.

I must have read it three times; I didn't really know what to do.

"Barney, it says here that the project is 97% complete." He nodded.

"But the project isn't anywhere near that number." He shrugged.

And then we just sat there for what seemed like a long time.

"Would you mind my taking this with me, or making a copy?" No, Barney said, that wouldn't be a good idea. And with that, I was ushered out the door.

I'd never knowingly faced a felon before, and I remember feeling really shaky going down the stairs.

Barney had signed off on the project as being essentially done, when it was nowhere near completion. The bank was saying they trusted Barney, it was his job to handle the signoff, and they had indeed given Ben what must have been a wheelbarrow of cash as a result.

It's hard to explain how I felt as this investigation deepened: not only did I not know who to trust, but I really didn't know if some of the players were serious criminals, watching to see what I was going to do about it.

Pattern Recognition

We were running this story on the front page, with a new installment every week. My "two weeks" replacing Brad had turned into months, since his return had no effect on my ongoing work on this front-page series, and the layers of the onion continued to get more interesting. But I'd hit another dead end: Now that I'd found Barney to be one of the likely felons, what came next?

I had one other lead, of sorts, which began with the question: How could a bank officer who sat 100 feet in front of a half-finished shopping mall agree to pay an enormous amount of money to the developer upon completion – when all he had to do was look out the window to see it wasn't true?

There's that "bank" word again.

If Ben's patterns in leaving the project didn't make much sense, the bank's patterns in watching him go made even less.

With not much more than basic math and pure guesswork (the bank had stopped being helpful), I figured Ben had left town that night with as much as $500,000 in cash – more or less, depending on Barney's potential cut.

I spent a lot of time looking up records on Ben, the bank, and the project without much result, until, one afternoon, I found a pattern that made absolutely no sense.

It seemed as though Queen City had loaned Ben the construction money, in approved chunks, based on progress. But there were no good records in our county about the mortgage or ownership; all the records referred to a different county nearby. I took the two-hour ferry trip, and sure enough, there they were.

Twice.

There was a shell company of some kind, and the mortgage (or something like it) had passed between the shell company and the bank over the course of just a few minutes. Even more interesting, it looked like the shell company had bought the land for the mall outright.

As naïve and new to the world of real estate as I was, still I could see that something was wrong. Luckily, I knew just enough about savings and loans (also called "thrifts") to know they were prevented by law from doing things like trading in stocks or investing directly in risky projects – like shopping malls.

Everything started to fall into place. When Ben skipped town with the money, the bank foreclosed on the project, becoming the owner of the most important commercial development in town. The land was transferred from the bank's shell company to the bank itself. While it was not legally allowed to build a mall, it appeared that it had used its own shell company to buy the land, playing the key role in the project, second to Ben. Meanwhile, the bank pretended to be at arm's length, hiring Barney to watch Ben.

This had suddenly become a story about bank fraud. And the bank wasn't the victim; it was the perpetrator.

Pattern Resolution

I knew enough to recognize that I was in way over my head. It was time to call in the cavalry. First, I met with the county prosecuting attorney, with whom I ended up working for months. Then he and I called the state banking commissioner and shared what we had with his office.

The commissioner's office told us to be patient, they were on the case.

I remember writing one more major story on the subject. It was perhaps the most difficult installment, because it named Barney as a primary accomplice in the fraud, suggesting that he had committed a felony. I expected that someone would have a warrant out for his arrest in a few days. This was tough, because I liked Barney – who didn't? I knew his family, I was friends with his kids . . . it went on and on.

But I felt that I had to write the story. If no one did anything about it at that point, that wasn't my problem. We published it, on the front page.

There was one more tough decision to make. While I suspected that the local bank manager – let's call him "Tommy" – had been involved, I had no proof; only the question of how he could have missed looking out that window. All the legal documents involved his bosses – the guys running the parent banking company – so I focused on them instead. I'll admit, here and now, that I let Tommy walk. I never wrote about him by name, and he was never charged with a crime.

Being a bit impatient, I then sent everything I had to a reporter at a Seattle newspaper, since Queen City's parent operations were located there. In addition to copies of all of the stories we had run, I included a short note: "If this isn't outright fraud, I'll eat my fishing shorts."

Luckily, he pursued the matter, looking into and writing about the bank's operations in both Washington and Texas. There was, it turned out, more, much more to the story. The bank had been in trouble and was doing all kinds of illegal things, beyond what I'd unearthed, to stay afloat.

By this time, everyone had "lawyered up," and we'd moved from the investigative phase of this strange experience into what you might call the "earthquake" phase.

Soon after, the Seattle paper having done its job, the whole Queen City operation was shuttered, in both Texas and Washington. Our local branch simply closed one day, never to open again.

The president of the parent company and two board members were charged and, after a bit, were convicted in federal court, paid large fines, and served time in prison.

While none of us could have known it at the time, this became the first federal conviction in what was later called the US Savings and Loan Scandal, the largest American bank scandal in history.

There were lots of pieces to pick up. Most of the small subcontractors – the honest people – went bankrupt. Some got paid back through a deal with the title company. And the whole project was set to be auctioned off to the lowest bidder, on the county courthouse steps. I got a phone call, just before the auction – very low key, and very threatening.

I skipped the auction. I'd done my work already.

Chapter 8

Inside China: A Strange Story of Patterns and Mathematics

I had a few reasons to go to China. I wanted to see if we could find a manufacturer or two interested in making a new computer for K-12 education. My company, SNS, had already created the award-winning Spark computer with IDEO in the US. Our Project Inkwell consortium had been the first international group to combine vendors, teachers, policymakers, administrators, and students to address the introduction of appropriate technology into schools, and after seven years of research and design work we were ready to build something.

I was also curious about the country, and wanted to see it.

Above all, I wanted to talk with the Chinese about protection of intellectual property and figure out if there was a way to reduce nation-sponsored IP theft by China. I had seen a deep pattern of state-sponsored theft of trade secrets from the West ("innovating nations"), which later prompted our taking a lead in combating this global threat.

Through a Chinese American contact in LA, I received an invitation to go to Guangdong Province, accompanying him as a guest of the provincial government, to see China's buzzing tech corridor firsthand, meet with IP experts, and look around for a manufacturer.

I have a longtime friend who was then working for the US State Department in China. Learning of this, "Frank" (not his real name) came back with an invitation to go on a speaking tour covering central and northern China, sponsored by the US Embassy. My friend Sidney Rittenberg (once friends with – and occasional translator for – Mao, who had subsequently put him in solitary confinement for 16 years) then arranged a private meeting with the chairman of China Mobile in Beijing. Dan, my LA contact, brought another couple of travelers along for the Guangdong trip, including a Silicon Valley exec and an expert in trade with China. Sidney's daughter Jenny offered to be my translator and all-around interlocutor during the Guangdong visits.

The trip to China was on.

Before I left, a top officer of the world's largest software company (let's call him "Jim") came to the island for our annual tradition of meeting over dinner. Jim would bring his boat up, and we'd chat on the boat and then go to dinner in town. Jim was also this large software company's primary top-level contact person for China.

By now, I had identified some real problems with the idea of getting China to stop stealing, or even to start protecting, IP. The most obvious: the leaders of China (and their teams of propagandists, who were quite good) were saying one set of things and doing the opposite. They were claiming, for example, that IP protection was improving daily, when in fact the rate of theft was ramping exponentially.

I had figured out that it would take at least 10 years just to install a judicial system that would enable IP protection: pass laws, train judges, install courts, and so on. A decade. I checked this out with Sidney, who agreed.

When I met Jim for a beer on his boat, I told him of the upcoming trip and rehashed my concerns about stopping IP theft. All of the patterns in China's actions were leading to a future of increased state-sponsored theft of "crown jewel" inventions, I said, even as they were claiming the opposite.

"You don't understand," he told me. "That's not how China works. When the leaders of China want to make a change, they take a few people 'behind the barn' and shoot them. You'd be amazed how quickly the whole society changes after that."

I found it hard to argue with this insight, and made a mental note.

China's Patterns

The northern China tour went effortlessly, thanks to Frank. I found my pattern-matching instincts on full alert, picking up the most unexpected discoveries. One example: driving in from the airport, I noticed something was different about the city buildings. Finally I realized what it was: they have exotic, carefully designed rooftops. In the US, the tops of building are mostly flat, ugly places where architects stick air conditioning and elevator equipment.

But in terms of the marketplace, one of the first big signs I had that China was up to no good was its approach to the very hot global market for cellular technology. Qualcomm and Ericsson had invented and patented (and fought over) various parts of what was called 3G, or third-generation, high-speed service. The key technology was code division multiple access, or CDMA; this was the "secret sauce" for cramming lots of voice or data into the airwaves, and it was a global standard, adopted throughout the world so all phones work in all places.

The Chinese initially refused to use CDMA. Rather, they announced, they would have their own standards. (Later this pattern became clear: China rejects almost all international standards, as part of its "Indigenous Innovation" – IP theft – push to further its own companies, rather than foreign firms.)

China had apparently hired Germany's Siemens (avid for China's favor) to reverse-engineer Qualcomm's technology, renaming it TD-SCDMA. It was a complete rip-off, and it took China years to accomplish, eventually putting the country almost a decade behind the rest of the world with a key communications tool, all in the name of stealing from foreign firms and benefiting local companies.

Getting a meeting with China Mobile chairman Wang Jianzhou was a bit like getting a meeting with GE's fabled leader Jack Welch. At that time, China Mobile had advanced from being China's largest wireless carrier to being the world's, with about 350 million subscribers.

I asked Chairman Wang, who seemed like a very nice fellow, whether his company would be using TD-SCDMA. He smiled. "We have no plans to use TD-SCDMA, now or in the future." That was interesting; it meant that China's – and the world's – largest mobile firm wasn't playing by Communist Party rules.

We talked for an hour, about the future of global carriers, technologies, and phones. I invited him to come to our FiRe conference, and he declined, politely. "I am only allowed to leave China four times a year," he said, explaining that the higher you are in the Party, the fewer permissions you get to travel outside China.

When the hour was up, I shook hands with Wang Jianzhou, his VP, and the other nameless fellow in the meeting (Party representative? Spy?). I would never see Chairman Wang again. He fell out of touch, and then was rumored to be out of Party favor. He left his post. After a while, China Mobile reversed course and adopted TD-SCDMA as one of its protocols. Today, rumor has it that Wang has been imprisoned. Perhaps he wasn't quick enough to use stolen foreign technology.

Talking to the North

The speaking tour in northern China went well. We visited universities in five cities. In each, I'd first have a very formal meeting with the university leaders, orchestrated by Frank. These would invariably be held in a long room, with chairs along the side walls for all of the entourage and two chairs at the end for the principals, usually separated by a small table, often with a beautiful backdrop. I would sit in one chair, and the president of the university would sit in the other.

Then we'd talk.

Later, I'd give a speech to a roomful of students and faculty and then answer their questions. The main subject of my talks was the importance of broadband and technology in driving the economy, and the value of innovation and protection of IP. I was hoping China would eventually get the message that in the long run, inventing was a better model for its own future than stealing the inventions of others, and it seemed there was no better place to start this conversation than at leading universities.

There were two questions from that trip that still stand out in my mind today. One student shyly asked when General Motors was going to go bankrupt. This was years before anyone thought that was going to happen. How, or what, did he know? I still wonder.

The second question was raised after a talk at a technology institute in Dalian. A student came up to me, the head of the local Institute, and another nameless adult (Party representative? Spy?) standing nearby, and asked: "Do you think pollution is so bad in China that it will cause a revolution?"

I pictured myself in a small cell in solitary for 16 years or so.

"That's a very difficult question," I told him.

IP Theft and South China: "Shooting Thieves Behind the Barn"

In Guangdong, things moved very quickly. Each day was carefully scripted, from dawn until late at night. The week was a long series of visits, sightseeing, meetings, and agenda items, punctuated by ceremonious meals.

Finally, we reached the part of the trip I had been waiting for: a discussion with all of the relevant Guangdong officials on the protection of IP.

Our host company had selected a beautiful setting, in a lodge on a lake, in a new technology and industrial park. No one had moved in yet; everything was serene and pristine. The plans for the place were huge, funded by international sponsors, with living quarters, labs, offices, and landscaped grounds and hotels.

It was a little eerie being there early, just 10 or so of us, seated around a table facing a wall of windows and the lake beyond, no one else within miles. At our table were the vice president of IP Protection, his assistant, his legal counsel, a translator, and our small team.

The VP started the meeting after we'd eaten lunch, describing how concerned Guangdong was about IP theft and what his company was doing to address it. Then it was my turn.

I started with a typically American approach.

"What if," I asked, "you decided to make Guangdong Province the shining example, out of all of China's provinces, of really great IP protection? What if you passed your own laws and set your own standards, providing so much protection that anyone in the world would come here without fear of losing their IP? This would be terrific for your own business here and would set a great example for the rest of the country."

While our host mulled this over, our Valley exec couldn't contain himself.

"That would be fantastic!" he enthused. "Just think of it. What a magnificent marketing opportunity for Guangdong, and for China!"

I noticed that the Chinese team was being quite reserved on the issue. They talked quietly with one another for a few minutes, and finally the VP spoke up:

"We don't think that would work. We already have laws and fines in place that are quite effective, with serious penalties."

In my right ear, the Chinese translator whispered: "This is true, but the fines are really quite reasonable, and people pay them and just keep making pirated DVDs and T-shirts."

I thought back to Jim's image of executions behind the barn. Maybe, it occurred to me, I'm just not communicating well enough.

"I appreciate what you're saying," I said to the VP, "but what if the penalties were tougher?"

He talked to the lawyer for a minute or two, and then the lawyer answered.

"We've considered this, Mr. Anderson," she said. "But we think that the current penalties are indeed quite large."

Since it was obvious that Chinese companies and individuals everywhere were ripping off foreign IP as fast as they could, it seemed clear that, whatever the penalties, they weren't working. I decided to try one last time, hoping they would understand my meaning.

"I understand the effort you must be putting into this issue," I told her. "But I can't help but wonder if the penalties were *really* tough, whether then IP theft might stop?"

She talked to the VP for a moment and, after a few back-and-forths, turned back to me. This time she was not smiling.

"We have executed four people, and still the problems persist."

I made two mental notes. IP theft was a deep part of Chinese culture. It would be virtually impossible to stop it.

And I had a very interesting story to tell Jim at our next dinner.

China's Biggest Secret: The *I Ching* and the Ultimate Pattern Challenge

It was late afternoon on the second-to-last day of the trip. That morning, we'd visited the brand-new Science and Technology Museum, housed in a downtown Guangdong skyscraper. Suddenly there was a change in the air: something was happening, you could tell from the talk among our hosts. The car stopped, and my friend the VP of IP turned to me in the back seat.

"You have been invited to a very special meeting. We would like you to attend."

I had no idea what this was about. There was nothing on the agenda; it was a complete mystery.

"I'd be honored," I said.

The car returned to the museum building we'd visited earlier. At our host's request, the rest of the team went back to the hotel, but Dan from our team was allowed to stay, as my translator. We piled back into the elevator, but this time passed the museum levels to a higher floor.

When the doors opened, I couldn't believe my eyes. Unlike the bustling museum floors below, my first impression was that this level was unfinished. Everything was cement: floor, pillars, outside walls. And then I saw it.

One hundred yards to our left, inside this gigantic empty sky-scraper floor, was a life-size re-creation of a tiny Chinese village, complete with pagoda. As we got closer, I could see that there were lights on in the main building.

Inside was a U-shaped conference table where four or five new faces were awaiting our arrival. A projection wall closed the "U," behind which was a small kitchen. Dan and I were served water, and our new host made introductions.

"We have decided to share a very important secret with you," he began. "We hope you will not share this with others. We consider it to be a national treasure of China." Then he introduced the other attendees: a Hong Kong real-estate tycoon I had recently met, two university professors, and the Chinese national expert on the *I Ching*.

What?

Having practiced the *I Ching* on and off since my best friend and I discovered it in the fourth grade, I knew how important it was to the Chinese. Historically and culturally, it was *everything*.[1]

The important thing to understand is that the *I Ching* is based on patterns. Knowing this will help you understand exactly what happened next. In fact, you might say that for the Chinese, and for many other people in the world, the *I Ching* is the epitome of patterns interpreted from nature, reflected into human affairs.

Why is the Chinese national expert on the *I Ching* sitting in this room? I wondered. What kind of meeting is this?

It quickly turned out that the other two professors specialized in mathematics and physics. Without much fanfare, our new host began his presentation. The lights went down, a projector began throwing slide images on the front wall, and we sat back. The experience was already more than surreal.

Every slide depicted advanced mathematics. No English, no Chinese, no text. At first, I think the presenter said a few words after each slide.

Even for someone who's taken too many years of calculus and some advanced math, this was very serious stuff: a kind of combination of set and group theories, symmetries, and self-abstractions.

It just got denser and denser, more and more abstract, with each slide.

What were we supposed to do? The mathematics seemed to be setting its own rules, creating its own world. What was clear was that this was important to them, that we should pay attention, that it was a big secret they really cared about, and that it was an honor to have been included.

After about four slides, I noticed Dan, who was sitting in front of

---

[1] Paul O'Brien, *Divination: Sacred Tools for Reading the Mind of God* (Portland, OR: Visionary Networks Press, 2007).

me, slump in his chair. "This stuff is way beyond me," he whispered. Of course it was: it was the wildest math either of us had ever seen, as far as I could tell.

But strangely, I was having just the opposite experience. It was as if part of my brain had recognized the patterns in the presentation of this new mathematics, and this led me into a higher level of understanding at least its core. Even stranger, at that level I was finding myself impatient with the pace, wishing the slides were changing faster. I remember saying to myself: Either you're going to get this or you're not. And if you're going to get it, let's just get on with it.

I raised my hand. "Would it be alright if we went a bit faster?" I had no idea how many slides there were, and this could take all day at the current pace.

Our host doubled it up, and then I signaled to him and he doubled the speed again. Now we were doing maybe one slide every 10 to 15 seconds. Occasionally I'd stumble on something, but mostly I felt that I was getting it.

The presentation went on for perhaps 20 minutes. Then the lights came up, and everyone looked around. I'd been in a dream state, but felt as though I'd stayed with the program all the way through.

The host asked if there were any questions. I told him it made a lot of sense, and then talked for a few minutes about the presentation. It seemed to fit my work in theoretical physics, and I explained how the Chinese math might be applied to a more useful interpretation of Heisenberg's uncertainty principle, one of the cornerstones of quantum mechanics.

The room fell silent.

The other guests then started talking quietly. They seemed pleased and excited.

Finally, the host stood up, followed by the others; they thanked us, we thanked them, and we were led across the cement desert back to the elevator.

The Aftermath

In the morning, we met at a city conference room. My VP host came in, smiling, with his whole team. "We have decided that Mr. Anderson is a genius," he told the group.

"We already knew that," my loyal translator Jenny replied cheerfully.

He presented me with a gift of two ivory chops – seals – carved the night before with the names he had chosen for me. He told me the names and explained what they meant, and we all had a delightful morning together before heading back home.

Years later, I'm still a bit stunned and puzzled, trying to understand exactly what happened up there on the eighth floor. Whatever it was, it was all about pattern recognition and discovery, when applied to mathematics.

Chapter 9

Currency Wars and Deciphering the Chinese Economy

It's amazing how differently the "real world" works than what we've been taught.

The wonderful thing about patterns is that they are *real*. Patterns emerge from nature exactly as it is. They aren't part of a theory or a book. They aren't political or emotional or partisan. They just are. This is why studying patterns is the straightest path to making accurate predictions.

You could've attended the best schools, studied economics, and then worked in the City of London for 10 years in foreign exchange, and you likely would've learned nothing to prepare you for modern currency wars. In fact, a web search on the term "currency wars" seems to confirm that I was the first to use it in a modern setting, in 2004.

Today, I have issues of everything from *The Economist* to *The New York Times* with these words emblazoned on the cover in large fonts. It's everywhere; the word is out. But when I first wrote about currency wars, few had seen what the world economy was about to experience for the next couple of decades, as nation after nation fought for the cheapest currency, driven by China's lead.

What were the early clues? They came from looking at patterns in our old friend the yen/dollar ratio, and by starting to look at China and its national business model.

The Yen/Dollar Ratio: An Economic Rosetta Stone

Japan has always held an interest for me, but probably not for the reasons it may for most Americans. It's not because it is beautiful, or different, or ancient, although it is all of those things. I've always been interested in Japan because of its contradictions: it is almost never what it first seems.

I started focusing on Japan in 1995, with the launch of our *Strategic News Service Technology Letter* (since renamed the *SNS Global Report on Technology and the Economy*). The US was the source of almost all technology invention, and investing, at that time, but Japan was the second-largest market.

Later I created a theory describing global technology trading patterns, which I called Hyperstructural Economics. This was a breakthrough, connecting what one finds in the guts of computers and phones to the rise and fall of companies, and to the trading patterns of nations.

I had found some simple patterns that I used as almost a mantra to describe everything in economics. First, the US led the global economy. Second, technology drove the US economy. Simple is good.

But Japan's market prominence meant I'd have to improve my understanding of the country – its politics, its leaders' personalities, its domestic and export markets, and its global influence – so that I could more accurately predict, say, the number of chips or computers that would be sold there that year.

My sole economics course at Stanford did little to prepare me for what I was about to learn from a country that was, at the time, the most advanced mercantilist nation in the world. I didn't even know the definition of "mercantilist" then.

Today, I use the term "infomercantilist," or "InfoMerc," to describe countries that do some or all of the following:

- Subordinate citizen interests to those of corporations
- Steal or force disclosure of the inventions of other nations
- Make money almost strictly through favoring export companies
- Allow punitive pricing at home to support below-price "dumping" in target countries

Mercantilists always select target industries for domination, putting up structural and/or tariff barriers to prevent foreign firms in those industries from selling back into their domestic markets. And naturally, these countries artificially weaken their currencies to provide competitive trade advantage. Cheap currencies make for comparatively cheap exports – and the whole point of the mercantilist model is to dominate global trade through export success.

By constantly intervening in foreign-exchange markets, thereby keeping the yen undervalued, Japan has favored exporters – like Toyota – which have enjoyed an ongoing price advantage over US car manufacturers. Additional structural barriers in dealership laws have kept American car manufacturers from making much of a dent in the domestic Japanese market for over 20 years, even as Toyota and Honda took major portions of the US domestic market. It didn't help, of course, that US cars were not as well-made, or had lower mileage, or even had steering wheels on the "wrong" side of the car, during that period.[1]

The cheaper the seller's currency, the cheaper the car in the eyes of the foreign buyer.

---

[1] Scott Foster, *Stealth Japan* (Friday Harbor, WA: FiReBooks, 2016).

It looks, from the outside, like predatory, asymmetric trading; and the result always favors the mercantilist.

But I didn't know this when I first started looking at Japan. I did realize that the ratio between the Japanese and American currencies, the yen/dollar ratio, was critical in Japan's trade. If you figured out how many computers the Japanese would buy, but forgot to include the effect of a big change in the ¥/$ ratio on, say, Dell Inc.'s quarterly income, you'd get it all wrong. In fact, early on, founder and CEO Michael Dell had some tough moments as a result of his company's efforts to deal with this problem.

Given the millions of possible inputs that would affect the daily change in value of both currencies, how could anyone predict their ratio?

After watching for a while, various patterns began to emerge. I had never studied Japan, formally, and knew almost nothing about it, didn't speak Japanese, and had never taken a course on its economy or its politics. I'd never been there. But soon this began a decade of almost 100% accuracy in making yen/dollar predictions.

How did this happen? I found "Mr. Yen."

Just Follow Mr. Yen

Dr. Eisuke Sakakibara, also known as "Mr. Yen," became Japan's vice minister of finance for International Affairs, serving in that role from 1997 until 1999. One of the traditional tasks associated with this position is to provide the international face of the Treasury, including providing guidance on currencies.

It didn't take long to learn how Mr. Yen had earned his name: almost everything he said about trade in the yen and dollar came true.

Wow. This guy was a goldmine!

The gossip surrounding his reputation was that he was so close to the powers-that-be in the Finance Ministry that he literally had the inside story, before anyone else. It was even possible that he helped to set policy.

Either way, Mr. Yen always seemed to get it right.

Now, think about that for a minute. Granted, this fellow has top access to the Japanese half of this forest of inputs mentioned earlier – but how does that convert into getting everything right? How would he know, ahead of time, about an American action or event affecting the currency happening beyond his radar?

Even though Sakakibara had lived in the US and attended Harvard for a while, this just didn't make sense. Unless . . .

A bit more digging revealed the real story. There were two possible reasons Mr. Yen was uncannily accurate in his predictions of the ¥/$ ratio. Either he was the best foreign-exchange predictor in the world, period, or – much more likely – he (or someone he knew) was controlling the numbers.

Now, that was an interesting thought.

Universities were teaching at the time that currencies were traded freely in an open market. Speculators around the world bet on this marketplace being free, fair, and open, and something like $6 trillion or more in such trades were made every night.

On the other hand . . .

The patterns were suggesting something that was supposed to be untrue. Patterns, it turns out, can be misunderstood, or misinterpreted, but they never lie.

These patterns became clearer with deeper investigation: the Japanese weren't predicting, despite their appearance of doing so; they were controlling.

The Japanese Ministry of Finance, and later the (Central) Bank of Japan, was intervening in the ¥/$ ratio regularly, as a matter of national policy. It was literally part of its business model.

I was stunned. It was the beginning of seeing the gigantic gap between what's taught in schools about economics and how economies really work.

Predicting, in this case, was essentially unnecessary once you had this single clue: just follow Mr. Yen.

Today Japan continues to intervene in these markets, and that it lies about both the frequency and the magnitude of those interventions, using internationally accepted terms and excuses that provide only the thinnest of rationales for old-fashioned currency manipulation, would not come as a surprise to most people. We're living in a more cynical, and perhaps smarter, time.

But no sooner had I figured all this out than another big problem arose: Mr. Yen's term expired. And, for some reason, his successors were less accurate in their calls. Years later, I'd realize that there was to be only one Mr. Yen.

Meanwhile, I was stuck, but there was a little hope that at least the process was becoming clearer. In the place of an infinite number of random inputs creating a ¥/$ ratio in the foreign-exchange markets (traditional economics), there were behavior patterns that dictated outcomes. All that was left was to figure out what the people in charge in Japan wanted. Within certain limits, it was a safe assumption that they'd get it.

Find the Patterns, Or: So Much for Free Trade

The next step was to look for the deeper patterns surrounding this currency manipulation. Looking back at the history of the ¥/$ ratio over many years, some patterns just leaped out. First, there was the overall trend, up or down. But there seemed to be ranges – particularly when the ratio was on the decline – where the numbers would just plateau, or get "hung up," for surprisingly long periods.

It seemed as though these were the ranges the government preferred, in order to favor their export companies. The Japanese were essentially fighting a long-term losing battle over the increasing strength of their money, and these plateau-like ranges represented values of the yen at times when they'd decided to take a stand.

Japan's whole economic model depended on unbalanced export trade, and favoring the weakness of its own currency was, in the eyes of the Japanese, just one more tool in the toolbox for how to achieve this goal.

A cheap yen in the foreign-exchange markets meant a cheaper Toyota car or Canon camera when they hit the US market.

Never mind that this violated international trade agreements.

There was nothing subtle about these ranges. The first was around 148/150 yen to the dollar; the second was around 125/130; and the last, at that time, was around 105/110.

For a decade or so, just knowing the above pattern could've made a foreign-exchange trader a rather large amount of money.

Of course, all good things come to an end, and a long overall downward trend had pushed the ¥/$ ratio down to just under 80. This means one dollar bought only 80 yen, instead of 105 or 125 or 148; so the yen was stronger, and Japan had lost most or all of the illegal pricing advantage that had come from manipulating its currency versus that of its top customer. I would learn later that once Japanese companies had exported not just products, but also whole plants, this ratio mattered much less.

Even so, as someone whose career relies on making accurate predictions, I was able to benefit from one final pattern in this run: the ratio had never, in history, gone below 78.50 or so. This knowledge allowed me to publicly predict that the Japanese would intervene again – a prediction that was followed no more than 12 hours later by the Bank of Japan making a massive intervention, subsequently backed up by banks from the G7. Yes, at some point even the victims get worried about price stability.

In a world of patterns made and broken, this low ratio was clearly a pattern breaker, and it was the lack of strong Japanese exporter reaction to this figure that led me to a huge change in my view of Japan's economy today. Of course, the Japanese had seen the whole thing coming: they were, after all, running the show.

The subsequent election of Prime Minister Shinzo Abe was based almost exclusively on his promise to cheapen the yen again. As of this writing, he has brought it back to over 30% in just a year, to its prior government-selected "plateau" level, which was around the 100-105 mark.

So much for free trade.

The 1997 Asian Currency Collapse

On April 10, 1997, I found myself making a call that was – there's no other way to put it – completely off the wall.

I'd been making predictions about Microsoft operating-systems sales, Intel chip sales, the US versus Europe in personal-computer sales, and cellphone sales around the world.

A series of patterns in global currencies so frightened me that something had to be done. I'd figured out Mr. Yen and the Japanese game, but that was small-time compared with this.

The Japanese had been playing a dangerous game with their banks, and it seemed to me that the US (Fed and Treasury) had just undermined Japan's financial position. I suggested, publicly, that this had destabilized the Japanese economy.

Asia was at risk, I wrote, if not the rest of us as well.

Here's an excerpt from an "SNS: Special Alert" we published that week:

> The Nikkei has been tracking almost 1-to-1 with bank stocks during its steepest falls.
>
> Readers last week read about the troubles at Nippon

Credit Bank. As I suggested, the bank subsequently announced it was pulling out of all international lending. Yesterday, it was further announced that the bank would go into partnership with a non-Japanese bank.

This is unheard of.

The Japanese government claims that Japan banks hold about $200B in bad loans. In an interview last week in *The Economist*, a top Finance Ministry official put the number at $250B.

My figures, which are admittedly very rough estimates, are that there was about $700B in bad loans 18 months ago, and that perhaps $2[00]–300B has been written off since then, leaving about $400B in the best case.

Japanese interest rates are already essentially negative today; the government cannot lower them as a stimulus, and investors can easily borrow (if there are funds available) there to invest in, say, the US market. With new taxes coming online in Japan this month, the government is out of tools to work their own system, as far as I can see.

With European rates still low, the US is now in competition with the Japanese government for domestic Japanese investment funds (pensions, etc.). Increasingly in recent months, these have been broken with tradition and sought higher returns in international, and particularly US, markets.

The Nikkei index is now in the 17,400 range, down about 1.8% since yesterday.

At this level, about half of the top banks in Japan do not meet the 8% capital requirements required among international banks. As the Nikkei drops further, this number of banks required to increase their capital will increase dramatically.

Summary:

Robert Rubin and Alan Greenspan have created a serious problem for Japanese markets, which are now very unstable.

If the markets suffer real damage, this will affect technology company business plans, many of which are predicated upon a healthy and rising Japanese economy.[2]

I went home that night and said to my wife, "Now I've done it." This was a huge call.

"What if nothing happens?" she asked.

"Then I've committed Prediction Hara-Kiri, in public."

"How long do you have to wait until you know?"

I hadn't thought about that. Usually, I put some kind of timeline on a call, if I can. In this case, things had just "destabilized."

"If nothing major happens in the next 6 to 12 months, I'm totally screwed," I admitted.

In October of that year, the Asian Currency Collapse began. It didn't start in Japan, as I'd feared, but in a weaker economic satellite: Thailand. In retrospect, I suppose that makes good sense.

The failure spread quickly throughout the members of the Association of Southeast Asian Nations (ASEAN), subsequently leaping across to South America, as global hedge-fund investors bet (and won) against a long series of currencies.

For me, this was a complicated and bittersweet outcome. On one hand, I'd certainly done my job, if that job involved warning of an oncoming economic collapse in Asia. On the other, it hadn't started in Japan. Had Japanese problems played a role in the weakness of the Thai baht?

---

[2] Mark R. Anderson, "Japanese Markets Destabilized," *SNS Technology Letter,* Apr. 10, 1997.

I still don't know the answer.

But at least I hadn't totally blown the call.

And I was learning much more about currencies and their role in global commerce. I couldn't understand why no one else seemed to be paying attention to this part of how the world worked.

These currency patterns would be increasingly useful and important, and would help me make another gut-wrenching prediction, sooner than I expected.

Europe Splitting in Two: Maastricht and the EU Stability Agreement

By the 1990s, Europe had finally tired of war, and it was doing all it could to create an economic federation of states that would preclude otherwise-inevitable World Wars III, IV, and (no doubt) V.

To do this, it first formed a coal-trading union. Then, after a few more steps, it laid out plans for a European Monetary Union (EMU), with criteria for membership contained in the Maastricht Treaty.

There were four requirements to join the EMU, based on Article 121(1) of the treaty, which would lead directly to the shiny new euro as a shared currency for members:

1. *Inflation Rate:* Must be kept at more than 1.5% higher than the three lowest-inflation member states

2. *Finance:*

Deficit: The total country deficit must not exceed 3% of GDP by fiscal year end

Debt: The gross country debt to GDP must not exceed 60% by fiscal year end

3. *Exchange Rate:* The country must have joined the Exchange Rate Mechanism under the European Monetary System for two consecutive years, without devaluing during that period

4. *Interest Rates:* Nominal long-term rates must not exceed 2% above the three lowest-inflation members

In 1995, the treaty was just three years old, and there was hope and excitement that this new European Experiment would actually take hold and work.

I was as enthusiastic as anyone, from a political perspective: I admired these countries for their political maturity, their willingness to shed varying national interests in the name of regional and global peace, and their vision of replacing brutal wars with economic inter-dependence as a way forward.

On the other hand, I didn't see how it would work, and I said as much in the pages of SNS.

It seemed as though each country was like an individual engine running at its own speed. If you took away their separate internal controls – like debt, and deficit ceilings, and currency revaluations – they wouldn't be able to run as one. They would all continue running at different speeds, with the effect of pulling apart the whole.

I wrote this in 2000, about a 1996 prediction on Europe:

> Several years ago, as the Maastricht Treaty was being discussed, I wrote in SNS that there was a large question whether you could link these different economies and cultures in a deadlock arrangement, whereby the separate states had no power to use interest rates and related fiscal tools to adjust for their differences over time.
>
> Let's put it this way: what if one culture values lifestyle, and another work, and the first is less productive of goods and services? What happens if you lock these together, and take away the tools that might otherwise compensate for these differences?
>
> Or picture it another way: we build a model, made of parts, and each part has its own type of engine and wheels

and gears, and all are held together loosely by bungee cords. When we fire the starting gun, they are all going the same direction at the same time, from the same place. But it doesn't take very long before some are going fast and straight, and others are slowing, or drifting left and right, and so on.

How fast does the model go? Not very. (You could do the same experiment with Formula One racing cars, and get the same results.)

The euro has been declining since it was introduced, to the frustration of its founding states, and, no doubt, there are a variety of reasons, some of which I'll address today. But as the G7 nations meet this week in the wake of their first concerted currency intervention on its behalf, no one (with the possible exception of German Prime Minister Schroder) is thinking that its continued slide bodes well for Europe or the world.

Now it's time for a few predictions, and we'll see if we can get them out before the news itself.

I think Denmark will vote to stay out of the euro. I think Sweden will stay out as well.

And I think England will reverse course, and also stay out, with the London Stock Exchange's rejection of the Deutsche Bourse as the first step in this process. (Yeah, I know, the LSE will link up with some other Euro bourse later, but that's different). And suddenly, you are going to have Two Europes: a Northwest Europe of independent successful economies; and a Southeast Europe with a mix of successful and not-so-successful economies (including new entrants Greece and other Eastern Euro countries).[3]

---

[3] Mark R. Anderson, "Ultracapitalism," *SNS Technology Letter*, Sept. 26, 2000.

All of those calls have now come to pass. Denmark voted to stay out; so did Sweden. Britain did indeed reverse course and got out. Greece, a not-so-successful new member, is now the perfect poster child of this productivity mismatch.

And recently, Norway quietly convened a first-ever meeting to discuss "Northern European Issues," with invitations sent to the UK, Sweden, Finland, Iceland, and Denmark.

Today, Europe appears to be splitting exactly along the NW/SE lines I suggested in 2000. We'll have to wait for the final results regarding the EU itself, but the EMU predictions have all come true.

Seeing Currency Wars

As I mentioned earlier, I might have been the first person to use the term "currency wars" in its modern meaning: nations actively vying with one another in the international marketplace, using their currencies as proxies for some other kind of economic leverage.

Although I published this view in 2004, I had come to the notion in its entirety very slowly, over several years.

Today, it seems like a major problem, but no one in modern times had previously seen it. Sure, countries were always revaluing their currencies, and that was probably a very good thing. As in our EU example, countries do not all have the same productivity characteristics, and those that fall behind will eventually have to devalue their currencies in the international marketplace to reflect that fact.

That's how a free market should work.

Currency wars are very different.

When Asia – and, for a short time, it seemed, perhaps the whole world – was going through its currency collapse, there were two noticeable defenses that stopped the domino-like fall of major currencies. The first was US Treasury Secretary Robert Rubin, who may have also had a direct hand in causing the conflagration (see the

"SNS: Special Alert" excerpt on page 92). Even if so, it was his calm leadership and sleepless globetrotting during this time that convinced the world's bankers they had to pull together, and not panic.

The other, more evident, cause for the stop was the China Dollar Peg.

At the time, China was already operating with its currency, the yuan (or renminbi), artificially pegged to the value of the dollar. It was able to do this without too much controversy because the country was still economically tiny.

In other words, the government of China had already decided, as part of its mercantilist model, to avoid having a free and fair open market for its currency.

How did this peg work? First, the government guaranteed that the market between the yuan and foreign currencies, such as the dollar, was extremely constrained and therefore easy to control, by arranging for all transactions to go through the government. There were virtually no free markets.

Then, to enforce its chosen ratio for the yuan/dollar, the government would intervene at any time necessary, buying or selling yuan or dollars until the exchange rate hit the ratio it wanted. This process of constant, unprecedented intervention was the so-called "peg."

When global hedge-fund speculators began pressuring China, the next intended victim in the Asian Currency Collapse, the Chinese never flinched. Knowing that there was a very constrained market, and that they controlled it, they were able to tell Wall Street and the City of London to back off. After a short time, that is just what they did.

In this way, China, with its controlled, nonmarket system, helped save the world from a massive currency collapse.

I was starting to learn about China in my own way, not based on what the country leaders were saying, but on what they were actually doing. I was assisted in this process by the friendship of Sidney

Rittenberg, the American author of *The Man Who Stayed Behind*. As I mention in Chapter 8, Sidney personally knew Mao – as well as every other Chinese leader since – and spent 16 years in solitary confinement in China, in two stints, for his troubles. And he came out of the experience without bitterness. His life's dream is for China and the US to be friends.

So you might say I had an inside track on understanding Chinese thinking.

The Chinese National Business Model

I had already watched Japan for a while, and then South Korea, and was now seeing China create its own version of the mercantilist business model, right before my eyes. This included favoring its export companies, as both Japan and South Korea had done, by intervening in the currency markets.

But China had time to study these mercantilist experiments of the recent past, and to improve on them. For that reason, I believe, the Chinese didn't settle for just the occasional intervention, like Japan or South Korea. Rather, they decided that they, and they alone, would dictate the value of their currency vis-à-vis their largest customer and target: the US.

They would lock the yuan to the dollar and just keep it at that value in a kind of trade death-grip.

When this is described as a peg, as it often is publicly, it comes across as something passive, a *fait accompli*, perhaps even an act of nature. You pound the nail in once and walk away, right?

Here I must issue a word of caution: The Chinese are exquisitely aware of how others – particularly Americans – interpret their words and deeds. They have become masters of word selection and use, and of propaganda in general, and may become upset if we use our own terms for their actions.

Try referring, for instance, to "Communist China," and see what happens – even though it is politically accurate. Although all the members of the ruling Politburo are good Communist Party members, they don't want foreigners thinking of them that way, for purposes of controlling the argument.

In the case of currencies, the peg is achieved by massive, constant intervention in very constrained markets.

Which sounds better: "peg" or "massive, constant market intervention"?

In any case, this control and intervention is the opposite of, say, how the euro, the British pound, the Brazilian real, the Mexican peso, and the US dollar had been valued until this time – all of which were constantly traded in the huge, open global forex (foreign exchange) market.

From this perspective, it's easy to see why American manufacturers are frustrated by the yuan's value. They've been forced to compete with companies in a foreign country that is constantly jigging its currency to make absolutely sure there's an unending advantage for the Chinese side of each trade.

Most calculations now put this advantage at somewhere in the 25%–40% range, despite the yuan's slight rise over the years. In other words, without constant Chinese intervention, an American maker of anything would have as much as a 40% price advantage over today's currency values. (These vary, but always favor China.)

That is a huge advantage – or disadvantage. It's like bringing a knife to a gunfight.

There is nothing trivial, political, or debatable about this; it runs against global economic rules, creates artificial advantage, and leads directly to the impoverishment of the targeted country. It is a practice that has directly led to the destruction of millions of American jobs. It is likely among the largest contributing factors to the near-destruction of the American middle class.

One of the interesting things about these three mercantilist countries and their currency interventions is how long it took the rest of the world to catch on, and then to form any kind of response. Had they been watching the patterns more carefully, it would have saved China's trading partners over a trillion dollars in trade losses, and 20 or 30 years of declining standards of living.

Japan, after all, was at this for decades before anyone even noticed. As far as I can tell, the Japanese continue to mislead outsiders about the extent of this policy, which they consider their sovereign right. Aeschylus had the perfect description of the current situation: "In war, truth is the first casualty."

None of the mercantilists want to have a conversation about how much they're intervening in the currency markets in order to achieve unfair advantage for their champion exporters.

As usual, the United States and Europe are "fighting the last war(s)." After World War II, I believe that Japan, South Korea, and China, each for its own reasons, looked around and decided that, perhaps *because* of US military superiority, the next war would be economic.

And that is the war that we are fighting today.

A Pattern You Can't Miss

People who have not yet recognized this are often confused by what they see. Where did those jobs go? What happened to the middle class? How could China rise so quickly? Why does Japan, a nation in constant self-avowed recession, have so much money and dominate so many modern industries?

In 2004, no one was paying much attention to the currency side of this war. The term "peg" was doing its job, keeping China's massive, constant interventions out of the news, for the most part. Instead, the eyes of the world were fixed on how many Chinese there were, how cheaply they worked, and how remarkably fast their economy was growing, even as the US seemed to falter.

It was like an IQ test, and the US – the ultimate target – was scoring off the wrong end of the chart.

But the patterns were evident: as mentioned earlier, every mercantilist nation, in its turn, had used currency manipulation as a critical tool in gaining advantage over its prime export customers. Japan started it, South Korea joined in, and then China took it further.

As the results of this practice (combined with other self-benefiting mercantilist practices) took their toll on victims in the larger "free trade" nations, these countries slowly began to wake up to the economic pain that was a natural result.

After a few more years, the fact of currency manipulation was being discussed openly, by US Senator Charles Schumer, by the National Association of Manufacturers, and by others who had managed to figure out what was going on. Millions of jobs had already left the US, never to return. And no one had told the American citizens that this was not just another temporary recession.

In retrospect, the patterns that escalated into the currency wars of today are strikingly clear.

But at that time, the question that presidents and central bankers were asking themselves was pretty simple: Why should my country work hard internally to increase GDP by a couple percent per year when I can just shift my currency value by, say, 5–15% and automatically increase both trade and GDP? My country will get many times the leverage, with no pain at all, and the rewards are international and instant.

It's like a poker dealer giving you all white chips, and then, when his back is turned, you exchange them all for gold ones.

China's intervention doesn't hurt just the US; it hurts every one of its trading partners. Brazil's real lost 30%–40% per year against the yuan as it ramped its trade with China, and Brazil's finance minister was furious. Chinese goods are cheaper in São Paulo than domestic-made Brazilian goods – which is China's intent.

An American would probably shrug and say, "Welcome to

Walmart." Walmart is the leading US retailer, and almost all the goods it sells are from China. In fact, it is a primary Chinese distribution arm into US markets. (One wonders how the arch-conservative Walton founders would feel today about being the primary retail tool of a Chinese Communist mercantilist model.)

Since 2004, the leaders of almost every country have gotten the message: you might not be cheating on your exams, but you can be sure the other guys are, and your team will get slammed on international trades.

It isn't as though US and other international leaders, including those of all the G20, haven't tried to get China to stop. It simply will not. Again, actions speak louder than words – and the actions remain simple: the peg, in a very tight band, still stands at this writing, after 10 years of polite conversation. In a world made of patterns, this is a strong one.

What Does This Mean?

Today, many of the world's countries have followed suit, or are considering it, and we find ourselves in a currency war that's gone global. What does this mean?

It means, first of all, that we've dumped global capitalism. We're valuing our goods and services against one another based on manipulation rather than on their competitive value in a free and open global marketplace.

Wow, that's bad.

It also means that, as in all manipulated markets, the information sent back to the winners and losers is imperfect. Maybe a car or furniture maker was building and pricing its products just right. That is, until a 40% fake-currency–value hammer put it out of contention.

How can a company improve when another, similar blow may be around the corner? And what, exactly, should it improve?

Today's CEO's answer to that one: Move all operations to China. Trust me, it is oh-so-ready for you. And the first cost you'll encounter? Turning over all of your inventions – in other words, your intellectual property, which will be copied, subsidized, and sold back to your global and domestic customers at 40% off (or more).

There's only one side that wins in a currency war, and the situation is ironic at best: if the "good guys" don't join in, their country gets hammered. And if they do join in, then the world gets hammered.

Currency wars have revolutionized every aspect of the world economy, and no one has come up with a fix yet. As with many parts of the mercantilist model, this blocks the growth of those that are most productive in the modern economic world. For that reason alone, it will need to be resolved.

How Will It End?

I published the following predictions in the *SNS Global Report* in early 2004, just as I was figuring out that there was such a thing as currency wars:

The Dollar and the Japanese Ministry of Finance

I am going to surprise you with a small factoid that I recently acquired, and which seems to be true. The Japanese Ministry of Finance has spent more money on currency interventions in the first two months of 2004 than in the prior year. That alone should put you on alert that there is something new in the air regarding the strategic importance of Yen valuations, but here is an even more surprising factoid, which, assuming it is true, helps focus the mind.

The MOF has spent more this year on dollar intervention than the entire value of 2003 US exports.

There [is an] obvious explanation for this somewhat shocking increase in intervention activity. . . . The Japanese are trying something materially different from years in the past, and it is worth spending more than they are making in order to achieve it.

[I have] decided that we need to call things by their proper names: we are now engaged in a Currency War, but one with lots of fine touches that are a bit difficult to unravel.

Let me start by noting that, from the Japanese export perspective, the world looks a bit like this:

China replaced the US as Japan's largest export market last year. The Yuan is pegged to the dollar.

All of the major Japanese exporters have now moved their production facilities to China.

When the dollar strengthens, it also strengthens the Yuan vs. the Yen, increasing Chinese imports of Japanese goods, while giving Japan the same edge it gains on the dollar in international export markets.

Simultaneously, an increase in the Yen/dollar figure, given Europe's lack of enthusiasm for interest rate changes, means Japan can increase exports there as well; and, indeed, the Japanese are increasing both total export levels, and export share, into the EU in the last couple of quarters, with cars perhaps a leading indicator.

Finally, forcing a higher dollar in currency markets, arguably, will ultimately create an interest rate hike in the US, cutting off the Refi Fever there and causing what could be real economic distress. Just as the Fed can create international investment inflows by raising the federal funds rate, the Japanese can try to play this game backwards, elevating the value of the dollar on the international market and hoping it will raise Treasury interest rates at the next bond auction.

Summary: I strongly suspect that the radical increase in Japanese intervention (over $300B in January and February) represents a new global strategy which leverages China as a springboard market, artificially strengthens the euro and helps Japanese exports there, and both increases US imports of Japanese goods while pressuring local rates higher.

It appears that Japan's dollar interventions are now focused more upon China than the US. If this also represents an attempt at control of US domestic economic issues, it puts currency trading into a new, more invasive light.[4]

When you look at global trade through the lens of manipulating currencies, suddenly everything looks different. It isn't a fair fight; it's just a fight. And victory – in the form of manufacturing plants, jobs, and trade balance (money) – will go to the country that cheats most. Every time.

So what can we say about things to come, given this understanding of how international trade is affected by currency manipulation?

The patterns are clear: while most other nations sit on the sidelines, all the mercantilist nations are increasing their stakes in the new poker game of artificially lowering their currency values.

This "game" is so important to Japan that the government spent more on it in the first two months of 2004 than the combined value of all US exports in 2003! And that was during a time when the US was its prime customer.

By every indication, China now spends more than Japan on this

---

[4] Mark R. Anderson, "The Swing to Asia," *SNS Technology Letter,* Mar. 11, 2004

cheat. And don't forget: while the Japanese intervene every month or two, as markets seem to require, the Chinese intervene daily. (I haven't spent time here on South Korea, but it, too, intervenes actively in currency markets on behalf of the won.)

It would be safe to assume that these patterns will continue for a long time, as long as other nations "allow" them, and given that such practice may be claimed to represent an issue of sovereignty.

If so, the tilted playing field resulting from manipulation will continue to give a global trade advantage to Japan, South Korea, and China. Balance-of-trade payments and accounts will continue to favor the manipulator nations.

At some stage during the destruction of their economies, non-manipulator nations will go beyond just objecting verbally and take action. This is exactly what happened to Japan after that country had already managed to appropriate US industries in television, steel, cars, copiers, printers, video cameras and players, and DRAM memory chips.

Just before Intel joined the league of bankrupted US companies, the American government brought a Super 301[5] anti-dumping charge against Japan, and the whole mercantilist train stopped. The business and government leaders of Japan immediately recognized a threat to their business model. It turned out that if we put tariffs on the products in the industries they had chosen to dominate, even currency manipulation would not achieve their goals.

Their response was brilliant, and quick. Within a few years, Toyota and Honda had constructed US-based manufacturing facilities, soon to be followed by other export firms.

---

[5] "Super 301 is a section of the law that enables the Trade Representative to single out a country as an unfair trader, begin trade negotiations with that country and, if the negotiations do not conclude to America's satisfaction, impose sanctions." "Super 301's Big Bite Flouts the Rules," *The New York Times* (June 4, 1989), http://www.nytimes.com/1989/06/04/business/business-forum-japanese-american-trade-super-301-s-big-bite-flouts-the-rules.html.

These facilities were Japan-owned, often did not pay local taxes, and generally didn't allow unions. Theoretically, the profits flowed back to Japan; and the US workers, many fired from jobs destroyed by foreign firms' "dumping" activities against their past employers, were happy to have a job.

I mention this more advanced, geographically spread form of mercantilism now because we will need it for predicting. We've seen a strong pattern, and the result of it having been discovered by its "victims." Therefore, we can expect more of this behavior in the future, from other mercantilists, also to avoid tariff protection.

This means that the US should prepare for a rather massive wave of Chinese (and perhaps South Korean) factories to be built on this side of the water.

But weren't low wages China's primary advantage in the global marketplace? I used to think that, too, until I understood how the Chinese model really worked.

This understanding would lead us to another prediction: Today, there are many countries (such as Vietnam) with lower wages than China, but I predict that these will have very little impact on China's business model or long-term growth.

The world has reached the point where those running national economies can't go forward without understanding China's model. World leaders now have to understand the Chinese through their actions, by examining the patterns they create, not through their claims or denials.

The leaders of non-mercantilist nations really have no choice but to come to grips with this more advanced form of economic warfare. Nor do they have much time.

The real answer, in this post–Information Age, is innovation. And it turns out that this is where pattern recognition makes its greatest contributions.

Part 3

Using Patterns to Predict (and Perhaps Improve) the Future

Chapter 10

Flow Economics and the IP Map

As I've mentioned in different contexts, after the Great Financial Collapse finally took place in 2007/2008, the *Financial Times* did a review and reported that only three people had successfully predicted the crash, none of whom was a professional economist.

Let's say that again, clearly: Not a single professional economist called the worst crash in history.

But those of us non-economists who *did* make the call publicly and successfully had something in common: all of us were looking at flows instead of balance sheets.

It turns out that balance sheets and income statements – no surprise – are full of lies, half-truths, and omissions. Flows, on the other hand, like patterns, don't lie: they just are what they are. And because they occur in patterns, studying flows provides real insight.

You can tell me that you have $20 in your pocket, and it may or may not be true. But if I give you $20, I know for a fact that $20 flowed from me to you. Likewise, the way to measure the pace and health of the global economy is in its flows.

When I first published this idea, in 2011 ("SNS: Rewriting Economics: It's All in the Flow," Nov. 15, 2011), I decided to call it "Flow Economics." Today, it is increasingly used by hedge fund managers and others who have strong incentives to get things right.

The more I thought about this level of patterns, the clearer it became that the world needed a new way to understand how the economy works – one that would be much more objective, and therefore allow for useful outcomes, such as predicting the future.

The path to this new theory, it seemed to me, would be through studying flows. This would be a complete "wipe the slate clean" effort, probably starting with some young prof at a major university, much as the Chicago School once became the source of much modern economic thinking. All I had to do was find the right person, someone who would clearly recognize the Nobel-worthy value of rewriting the foundations of economics, and – good things would happen.

The first step I go through in these situations is the "Am I crazy?" reality check (otherwise known as "Going to the Masters"), so I looked around to see what was being said by the smartest people in the field. It was amazing to me that the entire field of economists had failed to see the crash. I looked up the agenda for a think tank I admired in this field – the Institute for New Economic Thinking, which had just met in Berlin. Its top-line agenda item: Find a new theoretical foundation for economics.

One of the founders of the Institute, and a member of the board of governors, is Bill Janeway. He's also on the board of Science Technology and Economic Policy of the National Academy of Sciences, and he's perhaps the smartest person I knew in this world. Bill had managed the world's largest technology venture fund for Warburg Pincus while developing a reputation as a world expert on risk and investment.

Bill seemed to agree that this new theory provided a great new way of understanding how economies work, and he offered to introduce me to a few budding-genius types in the academic world.

I thought this part would be easy. After all, Bill is globally respected, and who doesn't want a Nobel Prize? Of course, nothing works as originally planned. I quickly learned that people on this career track were already pursuing their own ideas and agendas, and the last thing they needed was some crank calling up with a different approach than theirs.

I reached one famous young Harvard economist while he was shoveling snow from his sidewalk, by the sounds on his cellphone. He told me, "I can't change course to work on something new at this stage of my career. I probably wouldn't get tenure if I made that kind of sudden change." In other words, he needed to keep working on Google ads, or whatever he'd picked as a grad student.

But worse: he then explained what made academic papers and subjects in economics "sexy" to his peers. "They have to have a lot of mathematics – the more mathematics, the better. If you can't throw a huge amount of rather elegant math into it, it won't be well-received."

Nowhere in this conversation did he ever express doubt that the theory of Flow Economics itself was useful or correct: he just couldn't risk his career by making a shift. I started to understand what was wrong with economists, and how they could have, every one of them, missed one of the most important call in modern economic history.

No one has yet done the heavy lifting on this project, despite my best efforts to recruit some excitement in academic circles. No wonder people call economics "the dismal science." All I wanted to do was understand how the world economy works, using the patterns of the world itself as my teacher. I decided then and there that I'd never use the word "economics" in my own work. Everything we do now refers to the word "economy." "Economics" is a dead zone.

While I was working on using patterns to redefine how we should look at the global economy, I found myself diving deeper into all kinds of flows: foreign investments, cash movement, oil, coal, copper – it's a long list. Watching the global flow of cash, or "hot money," had helped me predict the Global Financial Collapse, but I was starting to learn a lot more about Japan, South Korea, and China, and their patterns were teaching me something surprising about wealth and how it's created.

IP Flows: Predicting Wealth

There's a widely quoted maxim attributed to Willie Sutton: when asked why he robbed banks, Sutton purportedly responded, "Because that's where the money is." Except he didn't say that. What he *did* say was pretty close: "Go where the money is – and go often."

I had been looking at the mercantilist national business model of Japan, which South Korea had later picked up and improved upon, and which China, as it turned away from Marxism, picked up in turn and drastically improved upon again.

These three countries' models had many things in common, but there was one that stood out more than others: stealing the most valuable inventions of other countries, copying them, and reselling them into the world economy.

If you want to know what's valuable, ask a thief, right?

Coming from a technology background, I didn't have any difficulty understanding that in this post–Information Age, technology drives the global economy. From seeds to tractors, cars to healthcare, there isn't a sector of today's economy that is not dependent on technological innovation.

I started by looking at the Japan of the 1970s, back when it was transforming itself from a seller of cheaply made toys to an industrial powerhouse. Some of us remember this era, when we were seeing groups of visiting Japanese businessmen, here on tour of US factories, snapping photos of every single thing. Americans weren't yet camera-happy. We thought it curious at the time, perhaps a bit eccentric.

In reality, as was later discovered, these businessmen were the vanguard of a national theft program geared toward taking and copying industrial secrets and processes.

During that period, Japan's government and business leaders, working together in a closely planned strategy, obtained American industry secrets in television, steel, memory chips (DRAMs), video cameras, and record/playback equipment. Japanese businesses were launched or ramped based on these secrets, which were turned into exports and dumped into the global market at low prices. Within a few years, all of these industries disappeared from the US.

Even the automotive industry was under siege; while it survived, the combination of competitive onslaught and stunningly bad management led eventually to the bankruptcy and/or sale of all but one of these cornerstone American firms.

It was a very impressive performance.

Until, that is, you reviewed South Korea's turn at the wheel. As mentioned earlier, South Korea did to Japan exactly what Japan had done to the US, stealing technology and secrets in the now-predictable areas of television, steel, DRAM chips, video equipment, and cars.

Like the Japanese, they used structural barriers to keep foreign carmakers out – even more effectively than the Japanese had. They just shut the door, period. And they used the US market in a bank shot against their Japanese targets.

The results were predictably jaw-dropping: within a few years after launch, their local firms had dumped goods onto the global and US markets far below Japanese pricing, destroying these industrial leaders in Japan and making South Korea wealthy. Their government and business leaders worked even more closely together than Japan's, and they won.

A Thieves' Death Match

Then came China. Of course, in Communist China, there's almost no line between business and government: today, the government owns between 80% and 90% of all businesses in the country.

I was working on this question one morning when I got a very strange email from a tech executive in Asia whom I'd known for years and who was aware of my work. His email included an attachment in both Mandarin and English. This document appeared to be from the Communist Party Politburo Standing Committee, the men (then nine, now seven) who run China. It described a top-down program for stealing intellectual property – inventions, trade secrets – from foreign companies and governments in something like 105 different named economic sectors.

Even more amazing: later, in an update of this document, the list was expanded to 417 economic sectors targeted for IP theft.

The behavior patterns were clear: some of the smartest political leaders in the world (almost all of China's top leaders are engineers, trained in places like MIT, Harvard, Stanford), from one of the fastest-growing economies in the world, had chosen to steal intellectual property from the West – from what I now call "the inventing nations."

To their way of thinking, IP was the most valuable commodity on the planet. I decided to agree.

In just a few minutes, a cascade of patterns all came together and made sense: the remarkable growth of Japan, South Korea, and – most of all – China; the slowdown and loss of jobs in the West; the clash between property-law culture in the West and copycat culture in Asia; and much more.

It was all about the business models each country had adopted, and then improved upon.

A few days later, in a talk I was giving to a group of business and community leaders, I wanted to explain what I'd just figured out. I told them I could give them the clearest picture ever made of the future of wealth creation, and it would take only a couple of minutes.

All they had to do was close their eyes, I suggested, and imagine the planet. Then imagine putting a red flag wherever a real invention is created, followed by a big red arrow from there to anywhere else that IP was moved, either by sale, theft, copy, reverse engineering, or forced disclosure.

The greater the value of the invention, the fatter the arrow.

OK, we're done. That map is the most accurate predictor of future wealth that exists. It isn't based on cash, or copper, or coal, or energy. It's based on the inventions and secrets used to make and manage those things.

Now that they had this mental map in mind, I asked the group to notice one more thing: almost all of the arrows move from places like the US, the UK, Australia, or the EU, to places like China, South Korea, and Japan. In fact, we could accentuate this difference by painting the thief countries red and the inventing nations green.

There was one thing in particular that stood out in this scenario – at the time that I was figuring it out, no one on the victim side was interested in, or doing anything about, protecting their IP.

If I had it right, half the world – the half that was getting rich – had identified the world's most valuable assets, and was stealing them in well-organized efforts. And the other half thought that something else – money, books, banking derivatives, Wall Street stocks, anything except IP – was more valuable.

This was crazy.

How could the Inventing Nations have missed it? Well, they had.

Many trade experts knew about the history of mercantilism – at least as applied to tangible goods. Others were aware of scattered cases of IP theft and the occasional damage caused. But no one seemed to see that this single issue could explain a global shift in wealth.

By following patterns, I'd stumbled into an ongoing economic war, perhaps a death match. And only the thieves knew about it.

Chapter 11

Curing Cancer

I had studied chemistry, biology, and then biochemistry, and had heard the story of cancer more than once: cells suffer "insults" caused by a variety of things – virtually all of them genetic or environmental – and then turn cancerous, growing out of control. Even so, it could take 20 to 30 years for this process to show up as symptoms.

I recall the first time this pattern was broken, as described in a newspaper report suggesting that cervical cancer could be caused by the human papilloma virus (HPV). Really? I remember thinking. That just doesn't fit into the old story at all.

So I made a mental note. If this cancer could be caused by a virus, could others? Why not? And how many? Some? All?

Over the years, this first finding was confirmed, and eventually a vaccine was devised for preteen girls and boys[1] that would help prevent them from ever getting certain types of cancer.

I could see that things would get very interesting if we suddenly learned that cancer was, at least sometimes, a contagious disease.

I wasn't sure society was really ready to hear this, particularly since the incubation period is so long that there's no way to know how or when you'd been exposed.

---

[1] Centers for Disease Control, "Human Papillomavirus (HPV) Vaccination & Cancer Prevention," https://www.cdc.gov/vaccines/vpd/hpv.

Meanwhile, in 2003, I was getting to know Nobel laureate Lee Hartwell, who was then running the Fred Hutchinson Cancer Research Center. I had been paying more attention to cancer and virus stories and had talked with a well-known geneticist about the problem. So when Lee agreed to do an interview at our Future in Review (FiRe) conference, I took the opportunity to make a bet with him onstage.

What percent of all human cancers, I asked, did he think were caused by viruses?

Lee thought about it, and answered that maybe one-third would eventually be found to fit this description.

I said, "How about half?" And the bet was on.

The Pattern Gets Personal

More years went by, and a family member developed throat cancer. Thanks in large part to Lee, we were quickly able to enlist the care of Dr. Waun Ki Hong, head of the cancer medicine practice at MD Anderson Cancer Center and a global leader in head and neck cancers.

I put my name on a mailing list managed by Stanford University for publications on this cancer, and it wasn't too long before I noticed a paper on the recurrence of HPV virus in a large fraction of the cancer cells in throat cancer victims.

The pattern was becoming clearer.

I wrote about the possibility of this virus causing throat cancer in our *Global Report*, meanwhile keeping my eyes open for more data. Soon, researchers were reporting that HPV was being found in other cancer sites in the body. A national vaccine program was begun for young girls, and it didn't take long for people to start wondering whether boys shouldn't also be included.

About six months later, Ki Hong published the first paper showing the correlation between HPV and some throat and mouth cancers.

Other cancers were starting to show up with viral causes.

At the same time, I learned that there are myriad versions of HPV – over 100, according to the Mayo Clinic. Most only cause warts of various kinds, but some can lead to other genital-area cancers, and those of the throat.

I was now becoming convinced that this was not a fringe story, but perhaps the main show. Although viruses often work in tandem with chemical insult (like smoking or drinking too much alcohol) or weakened immune systems (as during organ transplants), they were clearly playing a role, and maybe a key role, in causing cancer.

Lee Hartwell was kind enough to rejoin me at FiRe a few years later. At the end of our interview, I brought up our bet.

"Last time, you suggested that perhaps one-third of all human cancers would eventually be shown to have a viral cause. What do you think now?" He smiled, took a minute, and then dropped the bomb: "The number could be as high as 50%."

All the laptop key-tapping in the room suddenly stopped.

"OK," I said, "since I was at 50% last time around, I'd now like to suggest that perhaps two-thirds will be the final answer." And that's where our bet stands today.

So far, for better or worse, I appear to be winning.

What Does This Mean?

Well, the good news is: we can hope to develop vaccines for these cancers, if we know which viruses cause them. Eventually, with luck, we'll be able to treat people not only preventively, but after infection.

In the meantime, those working on boosting their own immune

system responses to cancer are, in my opinion, most likely to find success.

And the list of virus-caused cancers continues to grow. Here is the current status as of this publishing, according to the American Cancer Society:[2]

- **Human Papilloma Virus (HPV).** A dozen variants are now known to cause cancer.
- **Epstein-Barr Virus (EBV).** Increases the risk of getting nasopharyngeal cancer (cancer of the area in the back of the nose) and certain types of fast-growing lymphomas such as Burkitt lymphoma. It may also be linked to Hodgkin lymphoma and some cases of stomach cancer.
- **Hepatitis B (HBV) and Hepatitis C (HCV).** Cause long-term liver infections leading to increased risk of liver cancer.
- **Human immunodeficiency virus (HIV).** HIV has not yet been shown to be a direct cause of cancer, but infection increases risk of getting several types of cancer, especially in types linked to other viruses. These include Kaposi sarcoma, invasive cervical cancer, some kinds of lymphoma (especially non-Hodgkin lymphoma and central nervous system lymphoma), anal cancer, Hodgkin lymphoma, lung cancer, cancers of the mouth and throat, skin cancers (basal cell, squamous cell, and Merkel cell), and liver cancer.
- **Human herpes virus 8 (HHV-8).** HHV-8 is known to directly cause Kaposi sarcoma. It also causes some rare blood cancers, including primary effusion lymphoma; and the virus has been found in many people with multicentric Castleman disease, an

---

[2] American Cancer Society, "Infectious Agents and Cancer," https://www.cancer.org/cancer/cancer-causes/infectious-agents.html.

overgrowth of lymph nodes that often develops into cancer of the lymph nodes (lymphoma).

- **Human T-lymphotropic virus-1 (HTLV-1).** Infection by this virus correlates with a type of lymphocytic leukemia and non-Hodgkin lymphoma called adult T-cell leukemia/lymphoma (ATL).
- **Merkel cell polyomavirus (MCV).** Found in tissue samples from those suffering from Merkel cell skin cancer.

Now that we know that cancer can either be caused or enabled by any of various contagious viruses, it won't be long before the medical establishment – and society – begins to take more effective action to combat the problem.

While most people haven't come to see HIV as a cancer story, it clearly is. Since most of us are now aware of the potential for HPV to cause both cervical and throat cancers, adding to that list shouldn't be a great surprise.

The next steps, then, ought to be relatively straightforward: now that we have accepted the premise, it's time for research to explore the extent of this problem and to develop new vaccines and remedies. What if it turns out that most cancers are caused or enabled by only a small number of viruses (such as HPV) and their variants? In that case, you can imagine taking a few vaccines at the age of 10 and never having to worry about getting these cancers later in life.

Works for me.

Chapter 12

Equilibrium Genetics: Refining the Rules of Life

Something had been bothering me for a long time. I had learned how our genetic code, our DNA, directs the cells in our bodies. I'd also learned a lot about evolution, how DNA was only changed by things like cosmic rays coming from space, or very rare mistakes occurring when cells divide. And, finally, I'd learned that the ways in which these rare changes contribute to who we are today is determined by whether or not they better enable us to survive in our environment.

Some called it "survival of the fittest," although there was a lot of debate about word choice.

That, at the time, was the dogma in terms of how things work, how life functions.

It isn't that I thought any of these ideas were particularly wrong; they had a terrific amount of science behind them. Rather, I wondered whether they were incomplete. It seemed that there had to be more to the explanation of how life worked. If cells could get better at things over time, could their DNA "learn," or be in some way improved? And, even if this were shown to happen in a body cell, is it possible the same change would show up in the reproductive sex cells that get passed on to the next generation?

In other words, could our genetic code improve over our own lifetimes as a result of our experiences? And, if so, could those genetic changes be passed on to our children?

I had studied biology long enough to know that, if science were a church, these ideas would be called heresy.

The Viral Contribution

So, now I knew that some viruses can cause cancer, and that cancer cells are mostly just cells reproducing over and over, out of control. To make this happen, cancer-causing viruses have developed a number of "tricks," including using cells to reproduce themselves, and sometimes incorporating themselves into the victim cell's own genetic code.

That, I thought, was very interesting: a real pattern-breaker, since the dogma was that nothing, not a thing, changes genetic code, other than cosmic rays and reproduction mistakes. Now we had a third, much more common cause: viruses, of a certain kind.

This raised the question: what other exceptions are there to the old school rules?

It turned out that some viruses commonly leave their own genetic material in human genetic code, and that there are even cases in which the code of other nonviral species have been found in human genetic code. Is it transferred by a virus? No one knew. But the old model of a cement-like DNA was starting to crumble, with the one-way dynamic replaced in my thinking by a two-way model, with information flowing not just out of our DNA, but also back into it.

What Is a Human?

I am lucky enough to have a friend like Craig Venter, the first person to decode the human genome. Craig is a real genius and an amazing entrepreneur, a combination I've seen only a few times. He was the inventor of "artificial life," and now he's busy making new life forms to produce everything from oil to vaccines.

Craig was giving the opening-night talk at our 2012 FiRe conference when he dropped a bombshell that has already changed the world. "About 90% of the cells in your body are not yours," he told the audience. "The vast majority of these non-human cells are bacteria and viruses, which are an integral part of you, of what makes you human."

Another friend, Larry Smarr, was already famous in several fields when he launched a new career at FiRe; he's now recognized as the international expert on the Quantified Self, or the detailed measurement of our own bodies. It didn't take long for Larry to figure out that this community of gut bacteria and viruses was a key aspect to our health, affecting our immune systems, cardiac health, and many other things we thought were the domain of human-only systems.

In fact, according to Larry, if you measured the number of genes in our human bodies, it would turn out that only 1% of them are human; the other 99% belong to other species – most of which live in our gut.

It was turning out that a human being isn't just the sum of the human parts we've been taught about in school, but rather a community of species living together, from birth to death, specially fitted to one another in order for the whole to work most effectively.

As a biologist, I took two looks at the whole idea and realized that these non-human species must have been evolving these specialized abilities in tandem with our bodies for millions of years. They were likely as linked to us as we were to them, through a process called "co-evolution."

Suddenly, a bacteria or a virus was no longer a "bug," something bad that you "caught" and that made you sick until your body's immune system made it go away.

Rather, it turned out that the vast majority of these bugs are necessary for our health, including the functioning of the immune system, which we had previously understood as a means for destroying them.

We now had a completely new definition of *human being*.

Equilibrium Genetics

These discoveries had an immense and immediate impact on my thinking about how cells work, and how evolution works. After all, we weren't just talking about one species anymore, were we?

It turns out that a given section of DNA is most vulnerable to change when it's uncovered for use during a process called "protein transcription." This meant to me that there were at least two possible paths for changes to flow back into our genetic code.

The first was obvious: through viruses, which had already proven their abilities in this regard. Here, given that some viruses are part of the human ecosystem, the question became whether there are non–disease-causing pathways by which viruses could carry genetic information back into our DNA.

The second path was less obvious: since the cell had already evolved a detailed signaling and messaging system, a kind of manufacturing conversation between the cell membrane and the DNA, could it be that the more a section of DNA was used, the more vulnerable it was to change over time? And, if so, would the signaling itself be capable of being part of that change?

In other words, could the cell itself, without the help of a foreign infectious agent or a cosmic ray, make such changes to our genetic code?

In both of these cases, there was a great deal at stake in determining the ultimate destiny of the cell – and what drives it. Whether by virus or by organic messenger molecules, the DNA was getting information not only from inside the cell, but from outside the cell.

Could outside influences – things in our food, our blood, our environment – be affecting our genetic code?

Talk about heresy.

All of these patterns put together suggested a form of material – or informational – equilibrium between our genetic code and its surroundings.

For this reason, I decided to call this new theory "Equilibrium Genetics." Unlike the old model, it suggests that our genetic code is not cast in cement, but rather exists in an equilibrium state with the world around it.

While I had a new theory, I also had a couple of things to worry about: I realized there was a good chance I'd be ridiculed and likely dismissed by the old-boy system. And there was still a major logic problem preventing the evolutionary side of this theory from making sense: How could change to the genetic code in your arm, for instance, lead to the same change in your sex cells, and so be passed on to the next generation?

This was potentially a very real deal-breaker; if it couldn't be demonstrated, the new theory might explain real-time function in living cells, but it did not explain evolution.

But it turned out that while I was chewing on these problems, several researchers had been working on the evolution piece. Over a matter of weeks, two papers were published showing that genetic changes made to body cells can also show up in sex cells.

The very first pieces of the last missing step had been put into place.

I could feel the world moving toward this new understanding. It was time to go to the masters.

Going to the Masters

Naturally, the first person I asked about the feasibility of this approach was Craig Venter. Over dinner together at the 2012 FiRe conference, before his opening-night talk, I laid out the bones of the theory and asked whether he thought it could be a true interpretation.

"I can't see why not," he said, not seeming surprised.

Wow. Here we were, talking trash about perhaps the most important theory in biology – not to mention regarding how the cell itself functions – and he was apparently unflummoxed, just like that. I read this response as a very good sign.

Next up was Larry Smarr, who also seemed to agree. I started to think that either this idea was not as controversial as I'd imagined or the dam was about to break on this coming out into the open.

Not long after, my assistant and I had the pleasure of getting a guided tour of one of the world's leading stem-cell research centers: the University of Washington's Institute for Stem Cell & Regenerative Medicine, co-directed by Randy Moon.

Randy showed us around his impressive facility and then took us into a laboratory run by Charles Murry. Chuck pulled out a Petri dish of cells to show us: lots of little red cells, all pulsing. Then he showed us a short video of stem cells turned into heart muscle cells through a series of chemical triggers, starts, and stops. Suddenly, they all started beating – together.

It was one of the most amazing things I've ever seen: new heart tissue, beating heart muscle, being created from non-differentiated stem cells. I felt like I was seeing a large part of the future of medicine.

Afterward, I asked Chuck for his opinion about Equilibrium Genetics. I had to describe it twice; the first time through, I could tell he thought I just meant that gene *expression* might be altered by this equilibrium, not the genes themselves.

"I mean *structural* changes, real changes in the DNA, may be occurring in this process," I said.

That took him aback. I could see his wheels turning as he no doubt considered how far off the beaten track all of this was.

"It's possible," he answered. "In fact, there are some recent publications that could be interpreted to agree with your proposal."

We talked about these in detail for a few minutes; then I thanked him and left.

The Result

A week later, I published the first version of Equilibrium Theory in the October 4, 2012, issue of our *SNS Global Report*. It will be years before we find out if it is completely or partially true or false, but the patterns suggest to me that it is, in some way or other, true, and a new understanding of how life works.

If so, we now have a new theory of life, one that explains many of what were unanswered questions about how all life operates on the cellular level, and how it improves itself so quickly, both during each lifetime and from generation to generation.

Chapter 13

The Education Crisis and Project Inkwell

By the late 1990s, the American K-12 educational system was in a crisis. Everyone knew it, and no one seemed to have a solution. Or, rather (and much worse), everyone had an answer, with no indication that any were going to do the job.

And what was that job?

We were using the same teaching system (often called "the sage on the stage") used by Daniel Webster in his day – and his last day was in 1852.

Worse, the curriculum we were teaching hadn't changed much since the early 20th century, while the world around us – and our knowledge of it – had moved forward 100 years. Kids were learning nearly the identical material their parents, and maybe their grandparents, had learned in school.

And even worse than that, the system itself appeared to have been built with the sole idea of resisting change – including any form of improvement. After I'd learned a bit more about the state of education, I started calling it "the world's most effective immune system." It just attacked and destroyed any ideas from outside.

Did I mention that the entire decentralized structure was controlled by thousands and thousands of local boards loaded with well-intended parents who had terrific passion, matched with little or no knowledge, about education? Or that curricula were decided by committees of just a few people in just a few states – including Texas, where evolution and climate change were considered by many to be failed theories?

In other words, even if you figured out what was wrong and how to fix it, the task had near-zero odds of succeeding.

But all of this flew in the face of a single truth: there is nothing more important for the future of humanity than properly educating children. And so lots of people tried, all of them failed, and after a while, I took my turn.

SNS Project Inkwell

Like many parents, I began to get more involved with education when my children started school, in the early '90s. But the reason I went deeper had to do with the convergence of several patterns that suggested, after all this time, that we might actually achieve some success.

First, apparently without having given it too much thought, humans had recently digitized nearly all of the information in the world, from maps to books, paintings to music. Didn't it make perfect sense that any student should be connected to this knowledge? Of course it did.

Second, there was the internet. With increasing amounts of band-width already dedicated to schools, didn't it make sense that they should provide this connection between students and information? Absolutely.

Third, the devices were better. Inkjet and laser color printers could reproduce almost anything for pennies, and computer screens were smaller, lighter, and higher-resolution – and in color. The comput-ers themselves were smaller, faster, lighter, and a bit more rugged. They still weren't perfect, but they had improved enough to be usable. Almost.

One pattern that virtually no one but Steve Jobs had seemed to notice: students were going to be one of the largest customer bases for computers in world history, yet no hardware vendors had bothered to make them a computer designed for their needs.

Finally, most kids were already using this whole setup from their homes. In what was becoming a very uncomfortable, upside-down pyramid of knowledge, kids uniformly knew much, much more about operating computers than their teachers did. Unfortunately, in some cases this served to threaten teachers' authority, pitting them against technology at the outset.

Even though the timing seemed about right, Maine was the only state in the union that had created a one-to-one program in K-12, thanks to a very smart and very brave governor, Angus King.

I had planned a trip to New York City for a meeting at the tony 21 Club at the request of Hybrid Vigor founder Denise Caruso. I arranged to use the trip to add a few conversations with other people also interested in this problem. Soon three of us were having afternoon tea at Sir Harry's bar in the Waldorf Astoria hotel: author and education expert Marc Prensky; my German/Swiss/Italian/American friend and a European tech-connector, Kai de Altin; and me.

We were clearly, and fully, unqualified for the task – especially me. With a Twainesque lack of respect for this fact, we decided to take on the task of changing the American educational system.

Connecting Two Worlds

The main idea behind Project Inkwell was to create a global consortium that would enable, for the first time, an ongoing conversation between technology vendors and students, teachers, administrators, and policymakers. We hoped the result would include products and processes that passed muster with all these important parties.

In short order, we had assembled a rapidly expanding group that included most of the world's top computer makers (Apple didn't join, which was typical of Steve Jobs), chipmakers, and software developers. We then met quarterly for about six years, inviting teachers, students, administrators, and policymakers to brainstorm with us about what they felt was needed.

While doing this, we also researched who was doing what in this world, and we held meetings and site visits wherever we could find best practices, from Maine to San Diego. And it was in the latter that we found Darryl LaGace and Barbara Allen, and discovered the poorest school district in San Diego County, Lemon Grove.

Darryl – who went on to be appointed CTO of the San Diego Unified School District – had personally installed broadband wireless connections to the internet and Wi-Fi in the schools; and provided custom-designed and ruggedized devices for the kids; and, with Barbara's assistance, developed all of the training procedures to make sure teachers were at ease, properly supported, and successful. He had even cajoled Comcast into providing means-tested pricing for every single home in his district, to enable everyone to have broadband internet so the kids could do their homework.

It worked like a miracle. And all it had taken was a genius like Darryl, a human-resources maven like Barbara, years of hard work, a supportive community and administration, some extra money from Microsoft and other vendors, and teachers willing to try something new.

But price was the problem we wanted to have, since price always comes down dramatically once a new technology goes into commercial production.

With help from a couple of major tech firms, Darryl created custom-made, tougher laptops suitable for the real uses and abuses at school. These devices even passed the "Frisbee test": when thrown down a hallway, they'd crash-land against floor and walls and come up still ticking.

Teachers were excited, because, as one pointed out, this one-device-per-student arrangement provided them with more – not less – personal time with each student. "California just spent billions of dollars to reduce class size by a few seats per class," education expert Tom Graves whispered in my ear during one of our site visits, "when what they really should have done is find a way to increase personal teaching time."

Teachers also loved being able to see the screen of each student's device during quizzes and work sessions, so they could quickly get kids over specific speed bumps without including the rest of the class. It didn't go unnoticed that all of their aging textbooks were piled in the back of the classroom, holding up flowerpots, while the kids were online getting up-to-date information.

Most important, the students were completely engaged, working on science projects in teams, running experiments, taking videos, measuring outcomes, writing up results. They helped one another with math problems.

During that visit to Lemon Grove, I asked the math teacher about something we had predicted, but not yet seen. Since the model included students being able to go at their own speed in an Inkwell classroom, there ought to emerge a few "superlearners" in any given subject: kids who just roared ahead, based on passion and aptitude in that area. The teacher smiled and pointed to an achievement chart on the wall. Sure enough, a boy named José had finished the full year's math course and was halfway through the next.

The Spark Computer and the "Coolness Factor"

We still had the problem of designing the right device. Darryl had done an amazing job with limited funds, but Inkwell needed to create something that a major vendor could and would produce in volume, and that would reflect everything we had learned.

After years of research, presentations, and discussions, the George

Lucas Educational Foundation was kind enough to lend us the use of Skywalker Ranch in Marin County for a final all-hands meeting on the device design. Over the course of two full days, Inkwell CEO Bruce Wilcox handed around page after page of matrices of choices, and everyone voted on every line item, in iterations. He had at last extracted a detailed final specification, with all categories ranked for importance. (See http://www.projectinkwell.org.)

With this specification, any vendor could create a world-class teaching and learning device to Inkwell standards. Of course, we made it open-source, available to the public.

Finally, we brought all this to the kids themselves, in the toughest test of all. We invited our hardware members to bring in devices they felt were closest to the Inkwell spec. And, at a special meeting in Park City, Utah (future home to several Inkwell schools), we hosted a panel of young students and asked them to vote on their favorite devices.

We had entries from Acer, Asus, Hewlett-Packard, Dell, and a host of other hardware manufacturers. Each was a machine the manufacturer was already making for some other market, one they hoped was close to our spec and would fit K-12 needs. But there was one exception to this approach: our member IDEO, a design firm, had built a prototype to our spec just for this market, and named it the "Spark."[1]

While the kids were passing the machines around and making notes and comments, Toby Welch, founder and then-head of the Harbor School on Vashon Island in Washington state, whispered what turned out to be critically important advice: "Never forget the 'coolness factor.'"

Whatever the explanation, the kids overwhelmingly picked the Spark, leaving the business laptops forgotten on the floor. The Spark

---

[1] Adrian Covert, "Project Inkwell 'Spark' Aiming for OLPC's Head with Its Handheld Form Factor," Gizmodo, Sept. 2, 2008, http://gizmodo.com/5044598/project-inkwell-spark-aiming-for-olpcs-head-with-its-handheld-form-factor.

looked a lot like what one would now call an Apple iPad Mini, but with a keyboard, all wrapped into a single tough (modifiable for fashion) fabric case. This was, of course, before there was an iPad of any kind.

Grade: A or F?

We then took everything we'd learned about the process schools could use to successfully move into this new one-to-one world and put it into a single document called the AORTA [Always-On Real-Time Access] Manifesto, which we posted on the Inkwell website (www.projectinkwell.org) for any and all to sign. Our years of talking to teachers and visiting schools had convinced us that getting one-to-one right wasn't about technology in the usual sense, but about getting a new process of teaching and learning right – including the appropriate teacher training and support – in order to be successful in revolutionizing K-12.

After all that work, there was still much to be done and plenty of bad news to go around. Both Dell and Hewlett-Packard had decided against producing an Inkwell computer. (Today, a decade later, both make Inkwell-spec computers.) A host of other "copycat" organizations showed up – which was a good thing – and began competing for our corporate support (not such a good thing).

But here's the good news: the White House adopted virtually every point in the AORTA Manifesto, recasting it as the ConnectED project. (*Disclosure:* One of our members was head of technology at the US Department of Education.) And the Spark went on to be nominated for a design award in the EU and to be displayed at the Whitney Museum in NYC and in a design exhibit at the San Francisco International Airport.

Apple came out with the iPad and then the iPad Mini. Microsoft came out with the Surface. Dell now has a whole building of employees dedicated to serving the K-12 market. Suddenly, everyone's scrambling to make K-12–appropriate devices, all of which wind up fitting most or all of the Inkwell specs. Virtually every computer manufacturer is making a model that fits the open-source Inkwell specifications.

And many more K-12 schools today have one-to-one classrooms, with more coming every year. Even while some resist all change, it looks as though, at last, the dam has broken, and America's kids will get the education they need and deserve. Today, there are Inkwell-style schools all over the US, in Mexico City, and no doubt elsewhere.

Although Inkwell was composed of a small core team, we were able to get terrific leverage by timing the patterns necessary to make these changes possible, from student need to hardware pricing.

It just took about two decades longer than we'd planned, that afternoon at the Waldorf.

Chapter 14

Nutritional Microanalysis: Creating a New Field of Medicine

I've mentioned that I'd studied biology, and then biochemistry, extensively. On a different track, I'd also learned about computers and programming, and how to write software.

It turns out that important patterns often emerge when you cross different disciplines. While each area has its own strengths, rules, and patterns, something special often happens when you overlay one on another.

I'd had enough interactions with hospitals and doctors to know that neither gave much attention to food and nutrition. Hospital food was often a joke (want some Jell-O?), and, as far as I could determine, doctors weren't even required to study nutrition in school.

Head-On Learning

One day, in the 1970s, a friend of mine – I'll call him "Alan" – was in a near-fatal head-on car crash. When he emerged from the hospital, I went to visit him. Alan's spleen had been removed and, as a result of his head hitting the dashboard, he'd lost sight in one eye. He was told that this was the result of brain damage, and that the only thing that could be done was to wait and see whether his sight returned.

If it didn't come back in a few weeks, the doctor told him, it probably never would. And no, other than getting some rest, there was nothing more Alan could do.

As we talked, I also learned that Alan was suffering from serious headaches and finding it almost impossible to sleep.

To add spice to the issue, Alan was a landscape designer, just launching a new career as an architect. Two working eyes would be a plus.

I asked if he minded if I took a look at the chemistry behind his problem, to see if there might be something simple he could do on his own to increase his chances of recovery, and he gave his approval.

It seemed like the simplest place to start would be with the assumption that he had brain damage, and then go after why he couldn't sleep. Sleep chemistry was pretty well understood by then. There was a clear metabolic pathway involved in what we call "going to sleep," which was turned on by the signaling chemical serotonin. As serotonin builds up at night, we fall asleep.

This neurotransmitter has, among other tasks, the specific job of regulating sleep – and often, I discovered, of reducing headaches. A little bit of research revealed that people who suffered from migraines had seen marked improvement when serotonin levels were increased.

But I was in no position to tell Alan to get more serotonin, and didn't know if it was feasible from a medical perspective. Luckily, there was another route: figure out what serotonin is made from.

It took just a few minutes to find the pathway to serotonin, laid out in a college textbook. And its chemical predecessor – the thing it was "made of" – was an amino acid called L-tryptophan.

Now we're getting somewhere, I thought. The fact that a lack of serotonin could cause both headaches and a lack of sleep formed a pattern that was worth following.

The brain is made of nerve cells, which work by using neurotransmitters. It seemed likely that Alan's brain was also in the midst of trying to repair itself, with the potential result that there was a tryptophan – and therefore a serotonin – shortage.

Was it possible that in performing this effort at reconstruction, it was shunting serotonin or its precursors toward these uses, making less available for sleep?

And, perhaps the best news of all in this track of discovery: because tryptophan occurs naturally in many proteins, I'd be able to easily find foods high in tryptophan and suggest that Alan eat them preferentially. I got a nutrition book from the library, found a few foods that qualified, and arranged to meet with Alan. Spinach, as I recall, was near the top of the list.

"I'm not a doctor," I told him, "so I'm being really careful here. All of the things I'm about to tell you involve natural chemicals your body uses in making proteins, in foods you can get off the shelf. I don't think there's any way that following this regime could harm you. Of course, it may not work, either."

I suggested that he might be able to find tryptophan over the counter in the pharmacy as well. He thanked me and said he was willing to try. What choice did he have? Western medicine had offered him nothing but a frustrating waiting period for what increasingly threatened to be a one-eyed life.

Alan called me a couple weeks later. He'd had gone to the pharmacy, and while looking for tryptophan, he'd stumbled on that month's issue of *Prevention* magazine, whose cover story was titled something like "Tryptophan, Nature's Sleeping Pill." I had never heard of it being used this way, so both of us were surprised and encouraged.

Better yet, the plan was working: he was sleeping now – full nights of sleep, compared with having been almost sleepless before. And his headaches had gone from severe to almost nonexistent. So far, so good. He was eating a lot of spinach and taking L-tryptophan (the specific type the human body uses) in pill form.

Two weeks later, the sight returned to his right eye.

Today, Alan is an award-winning architect in the Northwest. It turned out that the patterns of his symptoms had indeed portrayed a clear path to curing them, if you followed their chemical paths.

Creating a New Field of Medicine

About 30 years later, I found myself in the enviable position of knowing, and sometimes working with, several people I consider the best in the world in medical leaps forward now under way. As mentioned earlier, these heroes included Craig Venter, Lee Hartwell, Larry Smarr, and Randy Moon, as well as Leroy Hood.

As I watched them individually creating a new understanding of how knowledge about genes, proteins, and various other chemicals in our blood and in our gut can be used together to understand body function and improve preventive medicine, I knew I was watching a revolution in health science.

But there was a problem. If I switched hats and looked at all of modern medicine through the eyes of a software architect, there was an obvious, glaring deficiency. Just like in a computer program, human health could be represented by three boxes.

In the middle would be the human being and all the species inside the human body; these were like the CPU, or central processor, in a computer.

On the right would be the "Outputs" box, where things like blood, urine, and stool-sample information could be studied, as well as body temperature, heartbeat, blood pressure, and so on – all the outputs of the human machine.

The third box, on the left, would be the "Inputs," which would contain our knowledge, on the same chemical level, about all of the things that went into us: what we eat, breathe, drink.

Doctors and medical scientists had spent most of their time on the middle box, on how the body works, so that box was chock-full of information. And then they'd used our Outputs to learn more about us, on both group and individual bases, from blood tests to urinalyses. So that box, too, was stuffed with published papers and detailed knowledge about the things the human machine produces.

But – amazingly – the Inputs box was virtually empty. We knew just the most basic and obvious things: Don't drink poison, Don't handle benzene or formaldehyde, Don't breathe asbestos. However – and this was even more amazing – if you asked for biochemical-level information on inputs, the box was basically useless. After thousands of years of medical history, we had forgotten to study the most important box. We didn't know anything about how our inputs affected health or disease.

Sure, every box and bottle in the grocery store listed its ingredients, as well as "nutrition" information: carbohydrates, fats, sugars, protein, and total calories. But very few shoppers seemed to read them, the lists were notoriously incomplete, and many listed items were made of other components. Worse, the foods hadn't been tested on a chemical level, so there was no way to know what was really inside those jars and boxes. Even more important: no one had monitored – on this simplest, chemical-by-chemical basis – what happened to people when they ate, drank, or breathed these things.

In fact, there was no way to measure what any of us was taking in, and therefore no doctors knew what effects these things might be having on human health.

On a chemical basis, which is the only basis the body itself experiences, the Inputs box was really, totally empty.

This realization astonished me. Why were doctors ignoring the most important contributing factors for good health? How could they spend a lifetime prescribing expensive – and often dangerous – pills, many with serious side effects, without first just suggesting a dietary change?

If you break your leg, eat more calcium, right? Bones are made of calcium. In the case of virtually every malady known to science, there is almost without doubt a suitable adjustment of what we eat and drink that will hasten a cure, or – even better – prevent disease from starting.

Why wait until there are symptoms, and real trouble, when we could just learn about what's in our foods, at the most basic building-block level, and adjust accordingly?

How much L-tryptophan did you have today, my dear? And how much mercury was in that delicious sushi? Well, we don't have a clue, really.

Going to the Masters

This seemed such a glaring error that I needed to check it with some of the masters. When Craig Venter had said he thought it made sense, during our dinner conversation at FiRe 2012, at that point I'd known there was something to all this. That first hurdle was soon part of a larger series of positive feedback conversations.

I visited Lee Hartwell at his new lab at Arizona State University. He not only agreed that the work needed to be done and was well worth doing, but said he and his team would like to be first in line to get the rough data.

OK, that went well.

Larry Smarr also was enthusiastic. Since Larry had been tracking his own private health parameters for a decade, and was now a global leader in this world of the Quantified Self, his opinion mattered.

Finally, to gain a bit more confidence on the issue, I decided to visit Leroy Hood, head of the Institute for Systems Biology and the inventor of genetic decoding machines. Lee was spending all of his time, it appeared, applying a systems view to health, measuring genetic codes in people and their bacteria and viruses, and monitoring a long list of blood parameters. In fact, he was about to launch a massive, 100,000-person program using these studies to understand human health and radically improve it.

I met him in his office in Seattle and laid out the basic ideas and program of what I was now calling Nutritional Microanalysis, or NM. He thought for a few moments, then smiled.

"This will revolutionize medicine."

Soon after, he joined our NM advisory board, taking the generous extra step of bringing in two of his own top scientists.

I was done. Or rather, was just beginning.

This new field of medical research and practice will take the rest of my life to really get started, and I expect it will someday be the prime contributor to preventive health outcomes when linked to the kind of work that Lee Hood, Lee Hartwell, Craig Venter, Larry Smarr, and others are doing.

And looking at the medical world with the pattern-vision of a computer system architect was all it took.

Chapter 15

Fixing Climate Change: Finding Graphene and Creating the SNS Carbon Trifecta

When I first heard about global warming, it seemed like the "perfect storm": it was complicated, at a time when the world has trouble moving beyond sound bites. It was slow-moving, when our species seems able to muster responses only in extreme, in-your-face crises. And it was capable of spinning off a near-infinite number of unintended consequences, while people were still arguing about its root cause.

Worse, it was occurring at a time when many world governments were taking their daily marching orders from corporations, and energy corporations were going to fight and lie about this issue without restraint. And finally, a large number of the scientific findings (such as ice melt) involved understanding second-order equations, with a voting population that was uncomfortable with the very word "math."

People have a hard time with straight-line problems until they reach crisis mode; asking them to take action on problems that get worse, the worse they get – well, it wasn't going to happen.

Understanding the Problem

Before deciding whether this situation was as scary as it seemed, I tried to find the smartest people I could who were conversant on the subject. (Seeing a pattern?) Over a period of years, we'd brought many of them to our FiRe conference and given them the floor. They'd described all kinds of discoveries confirming the problems, and shared new understandings of the many aspects involved, from ocean acidification to the insurance and agricultural costs inherent to climate change.

At FiRe 2008, venture capitalist Vinod Khosla explained his exhaustive analysis regarding the need for alternative energy sources; in 2009, the Scripps Institute's V.J. "Ram" Ramanathan announced his recent discovery that 18% of the global heating problem was caused by "black soot" – tiny carbon particles released from things like forest fires, diesel engines, and small family stoves in emerging nations. There was suddenly a lot to learn.

Our SNS FiReFilms initiative – whose mission is "to identify, support, and promote potentially world-changing documentary films in which technology improves the human condition" – hosted a great documentary at FiRe 2010, *Climate Refugees*, examining the millions of people who will become dislocated as the planet heats up. Where will they go? It was becoming a military and political, as well as economic, question.

During all of this, ExxonMobil was spending what appeared to be about $5 million per year on finding one or two lone scientists to continue the public-relations strategy first used by the tobacco industry. Under the rubric "Deny, Delay, Dither," the idea was to keep making profits for at least another 30 years by spending 10 years on each of these phases. Ten years in Denial, using the tiny fraction of for-sale scientists who'd play along with the bad guys. Then 10 more years in Delay, as the old "More study is needed" refrain played out. And, finally, having retreated from both those positions, there would be 10 more years of "It's too late to bother," or "What can we really do, anyway?"

ExxonMobil alone was making up to $10 billion in profits per quarter. You can do the math on how much money was involved in buying 30 more years without rocking the boat – and how much the company would pay to get it – something like one five-thousandth of a percent of its quarterly profits.

There were others: coal companies, natural-gas companies, and their various billionaire owners, any one of whom could buy every seat in Congress, if so moved. Worse again, the Supreme Court had again voted along party lines to extend an obscure 19th-century ruling giving corporations the rights of citizens. The Citizens United case, and another like it a few years later, opened the doors to levels of suddenly legalized corruption and bribery that would make US Congressional action impossible.

And so it did.

I decided that we needed a much simpler way to get the word out to normal people . . . something pictorial. We needed something so simple you could put it on the front and back of a T-shirt and the arguments would be over.

It didn't take long to figure out what these two pictures would be. The first was a chart of carbon dioxide concentrations in the atmosphere, over a long time scale, plotted against temperature. The two moved in lockstep, and it was obvious that both had gone from historic patterns in a tightly constrained band to a sudden jump, nearly straight up, as human industry blossomed and the population grew.

The second was even simpler: the melting ice caps.

ExxonMobil and the coal lobbies, helped by Fox "Not News" TV, could do their best to lie about the science and offer increasingly obscure arguments, but here was something you couldn't fake. Heat melts ice. More heat causes more ice melts. Ice that had been stable for hundreds of thousands of years was melting. A look at shrinking ice caps at either pole was proof.

How to Save the World

While we were researching these problems, we decided to hand the whole thing over to what we call the "CTO Design Challenge," at FiRe, to see what kind of solution that select team would come up with.

Every year, we put about 10 of the smartest people in technology we can find – mostly CTOs – onstage, in a TV-show–like setting first created for us and hosted by science-fiction author and physicist David Brin, and give them a seemingly impossible, real problem to solve. We invite more of the smartest people we know to be judges and assess their results after three days of all-day, all-night work.

Without fail, these teams always find new, outside-of-the-box solutions. It is amazing.

So, in 2010, we gave that year's group the problem of solving global warming. On the fourth day – the last day of FiRe – they reported out their solutions in an hour-long presentation. They had been asked to come up with a way to avoid more than a 2-degree Centigrade increase in global average temperature, which at the time was a threshold that scientists thought represented a kind of point of no return.

Their judge in this work was Nathan Lewis, a Caltech chemistry professor who's one of the world experts on climate change. He had given our opening-night talk on the proposal that it was now impossible to avoid a 2-degree Centigrade "excursion." And, in the audience, we had with us the scientist who had just constructed the most advanced climate model yet done anywhere, on behalf of MIT and Morgan Stanley bank.

They nailed it. The CTOs explained that a single answer would no longer work, but a response built of phases would. They outlined each phase, with a detailed description of how to achieve and measure it, and what the final result would be. They gave timelines and arguments in support of the whole process. And they ended by handing over a huge PowerPoint slide deck documenting their proposal, step by step. They should've called it "How to Save the World."

Contrary to his speech just a few nights before, Nathan announced that, to his surprise, they had indeed come up with a solution set. If we humans followed their plans, we could still avoid going past 2 degrees C. of warming.

Knowing how important this was, our staff then made a professional video of Nate's original speech, describing the science and the problems, together with the Challenge participants' onstage discussions and final presentation. We added the PowerPoint deck in a separate file for viewing and showing to others and made 535 copies.

We sent one to every member of the US Congress and the Senate, with a cover letter describing the project and inviting their response and participation in preventing global disaster.

What happened next?

To this day, there hasn't been a single reply. Not even a "Thanks for contacting us" or "We'll get back to you."

I think that was when I lost the last of my confidence in our elected government.

Another Path:
From Graphene to the SNS Carbon Trifecta

Since the problem wasn't going to go away on its own, it seemed important to think of a completely different approach to reducing global warming.

If the issue was how to stop putting so much carbon dioxide in the air, and if fossil-fuel energy plants were a prime contributor, then I'd start there. Clearly, any new solution would have to address the corrupting patterns of the fossil-fuel industry's lobbying work to block all progress.

What if this harmful waste product had a commercial use? CO_2 is just carbon and oxygen. Oxygen is good for humans, so what could we do with the carbon?

At first, making carbon nanotubes – already a budding market – seemed like the right idea. Everything from airplanes to tennis rackets were made of this amazing pure-carbon material. I had long been fascinated with the potential of all-carbon "Bucky balls," but tubes seemed more useful commercially.

Here we were facing a mammoth problem, much larger than the market for tennis rackets and airplanes, and I wasn't convinced that either of these shapes – balls or tubes – was going to provide enough demand to account for all the carbon dioxide being produced each day around the world.

If you could pick any universal shape for a pure-carbon structure, what would it be? If not tubes or balls, then what?

It suddenly came to me: what if there were such a thing as flat carbon? Carbon in sheets, one atom thick. Sheets could be any size and could easily be wound into any other shape needed. Much like fiberglass, they could be used with a binder; and in small flakes, they could be turned into virtually anything, of any size or scale.

After looking deeper, I found that just such a substance had already been created; it was called graphene. In fact, Andre Geim and Konstantin Novoselov had just received a Nobel Prize for its isolation, characterization, and production, and a few people had figured out how to make it usable.

No sooner had I found its name than papers started coming out with more discoveries of its properties and uses. Graphene, it turned out, is the most amazing material on the planet.

No other material is stronger or more capable of a mind-blowing number of properties. It can be transparent or opaque. It can conduct heat or insulate. It's the best conductor of electricity. It's almost as though, in our hour of need, a benevolent deity had invented a miracle material, and we could make it out of the waste product that would otherwise destroy the planet.

I published a proposal I named "Twinning," in which every coal-fired energy plant would be paired with a graphene-production plant. The idea was simple: make the fossil-fuel companies part-owners in the graphene plants and turn their deadly waste product into an extremely valuable commercial commodity. I described the idea in an interview with *Forbes*, which they posted online the next day.

Not only would this save the planet, on a chemical basis, but it would turn the obstructionists into willing business partners, eliminating the toxic and suicidal politics of the day.

But there was a problem.

Actually, there were two problems.

First, people had a hard time wrapping their heads around why, having burned carbon to create CO_2, it would then make sense to reduce CO_2 back to being carbon again. Wasn't that a complete wash, financially and chemically? What a dumb idea!

Here's a story that shows how bad this problem was.

A CEO had contacted me after reading my Twinning proposal. He already had a pilot plant in California that produced graphene nano-flakes out of CO_2, and he assured me that he could scale-up his process to a full coal-energy plant twin if the opportunity arose.

I emailed Tom Kalil, President Obama's science adviser – officially, the deputy director for Technology and Innovation at the White House Office of Science and Technology Policy – who, after asking a few questions, agreed to set up a meeting between this CEO and the Department of Energy. The next week, the CEO flew to Washington, DC, and spent all day with three top people at the DoE.

They agreed that this matching of waste product to graphene was technically feasible, and could solve the planetary crisis, but they thought they'd found a show-stopper to Twinning.

They could buy CO_2 cheaper on the open market.

I don't want to sound uncharitable, but . . . this was the dumbest, most self-destructive response possible.

If we were destroying the planet, then there was an added "external" cost to using their cheaper carbon-dioxide source: the end of human life.

In addition to not accounting for the external cost of destroying the Earth, there was another nuance to people "getting" the Twinning proposal. While it's true that it involves turning carbon into carbon dioxide and then back to carbon again, the beginning and end products would be radically different, chemically and financially. Graphene was going to be the most useful material on the planet, it seemed to me. Coal, oil, natural gas, and even carbon powder were less useful, and they cost much less on the open market.

It was like saying that pencils and diamonds are the same; or that fertilizer and opium are made of the same material, so why grow poppies?

We wanted to turn the lowest-cost form of carbon into a magnificent, almost magic form that could be used by anyone, to make anything.

Looking around, I realized that everything I saw could be made of graphene: the office furniture, the windows, the walls, the building itself, the computers, the chips, the clothing I was wearing. And when the clothing got boring (it would probably never rip), it could be sent to the shredder and made into an airplane, or a car, or a pair of contact lenses.

Isn't this obviously wonderful?

About that time, the Europeans got the message, and in 2013, Britain provided one of the largest research awards ever granted

– €500 million (US$670 million) – to develop graphene production techniques and markets. Almost overnight, the EU announced its own government funding for research and development, and exploration of commercial markets, which it then quickly doubled to 1B euro.

Somebody was getting the message. Hopefully, the White House was getting it, too.

I was asked to become an unpaid advisory board member for the brand-new Graphene Stakeholders' Association, which I accepted, and which helped me learn a lot more about the material and its markets.

There was another problem. According to my new CEO friend, the greatest challenge for him and other graphene makers was finding customers. While the rest of the research community was finding new applications on a daily basis for this wonder material, it was still very early, and it wasn't easy to find paying customers for real products.

Over the next year, while I was trying to figure this out, many new materials were emerging that benefited from being combined with graphene. Graphene had been used to build transistors and chips, new chip techniques were already supplanting year-old techniques, and new applications for graphene use were ramping at an incredible speed.

It was like the international space race, but for domination of graphene patents and markets – in other words, for domination of almost every single thing made on Earth.

But customers were still hard to find. The usual tier of high-end sports-equipment makers had already begun using graphene in their products, and I expected Boeing and BMW to come next. But we needed a better idea, something with real speed and scale.

3D Printing: A Solution in Search of a Problem

The whole 3D-printing phenomenon had been struggling for years. Yes, it was cool; yes, it was mind-blowing to watch the slow-motion creation – albeit usually in crappy, bland-colored plastics – of a prototype of something. You could copy a small part or toy, or make a prototype, but only in one kind of plastic, and it meant you'd be waiting around for a long time.

And things were not getting better faster. The world's top printer makers had moved from using one material to two at once; and then, finally, three.

Do you know how many types of materials there are in your phone, or computer, or car, or house?

This was a solution in search of a problem. Everyone loved the shiny new thing, but no one had a real market for it, beyond General Electric making one-offs of jet-engine parts.

Now, if 3D printers could be made that could take their weakness – only being able to use one or a very few types of material – and make it into an asset, things would get very interesting, very quickly. What if, I wondered, you built a 3D printer that used nano-flakes of graphene? I called my CEO friend for his opinion. He thought it was a real possibility.

Suddenly, the world of 3D printing looked full of promise. If you could combine graphene nano-flakes with a couple of different binding agents (glues and polymers, for example) to elicit different properties, you could then make – well, anything.

Commercial demand for graphene would go through the roof. We could turn all of the world's waste CO_2 into all of the world's new, sustainable materials. We would have the fossil-fuel producers as our business partners, and their lobbyists on our side. Commercial demand would ramp, and the planet could graduate from a dead-end, resource-exhaustion manufacturing model to one of infinite renewal and sustainability.

We changed the name of our proposal from Twinning to the Carbon Trifecta. Coined as a betting term, "trifecta" originally referred to accurately calling the first-, second-, and third-place winners in a horse race.

No one has built this yet, and, like the racehorse trifecta, the bet is a long shot.

But the stakes are pretty high, and each of the three parts actually makes the others more valuable, and therefore more likely to succeed: taking CO_2 out of the air, turning it into graphene, and then making a 3D-printable form of it for global mass production was the best solution set that solved all of the problems at once.

It also had the benefit of making money, which would accelerate a process that needed to be done quickly, while turning bitter enemies into business partners.

Finally, in the longer view, it enabled a "circular economy" based on the complete reusability and repurposing of a single material. If one needed a final foundational benefit, it also reduced the cost of research and development across all things made, after thousands of years of separate funding for steel vs. aluminum vs. cement, and so on. And it promised to reduce the price of this precious, renewable material by a percentage of hundreds or even thousands, as production ramped into the range of gigatons per year.

If you have to make a bet on survival, this is a good one.

And the patterns, at least outside of Washington, DC, are all in our favor.

Part 4

Analyzing the Patterns Behind Three Major Calls

Chapter 16

Calling the Great Financial Collapse

In the spring of 2007, it seemed as though more people than at any time in history were making, if not minting, money. Wherever you turned, from stocks to real estate, the world was getting richer. And while many investors later noted that growth rates in real estate could not continue, no one was very worried about the future.

The Global Financial Collapse began to bare its teeth in the late summer of 2007, and by fall of 2008 the world was in a terrifying downward economic spiral. While most pundits place the GFC second to the Great Depression of the 1930s, this is probably wrong: the GFC destroyed much more value worldwide, more quickly – but the world had the benefit of having been through a prior catastrophe, and so took dramatic early steps to mitigate damage.

It's hard, just one decade later, to remember the fear and challenges of that collapse. One metric that comes to mind: at one point, it appeared that the world's bankers had managed to create over $600 trillion in derivatives (securities based on specific economic events, often defined so opaquely that few inspectors understood them), all at risk – or about 10 times the size of the entire global economy.

The question bears repeating: How many professional economists predicted this most important event of their lifetimes? According to the *Financial Times*, the answer was "None."

What were the basic patterns like at the time? Pretty rosy. Here are a few showing the runup to that March of 2007.

The Dow was ramping up:

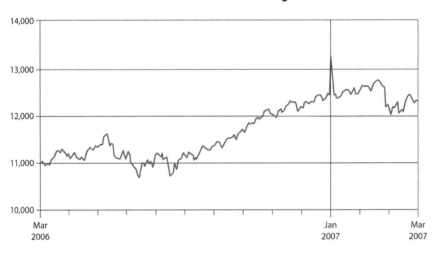

Dow Jones Industrial Average

Figure 16-1. Dow Jones Industrial Average, March 2006–March 2007. © 2017 MarketWatch (BigCharts.com).

The UK's FTSE was a bit more erratic, but not a source of concern:

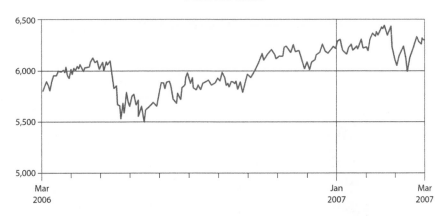

Figure 16-2. The UK's FTSE, March 2006–March 2007. © 2017 MarketWatch (BigCharts.com).

Global GDP was moving along at a steady pace, according to this OECD chart:

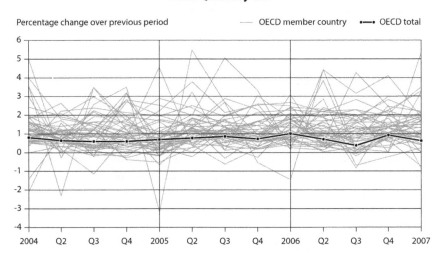

Figure 16-3. OECD quarterly GDP (2004–2007), showing percentage change over previous period. © 2017 data.OECD.org.

Real estate, of course, was booming. Here are some figures for that period from the US markets, in annual percentage-growth rates by price:

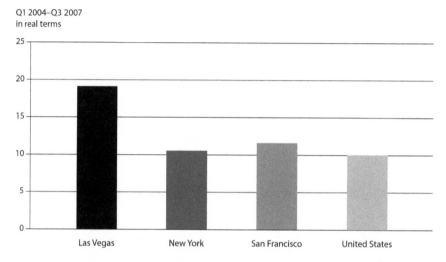

Real Estate Annual Percentage Growth by Price

Q1 2004–Q3 2007
in real terms

Figure 16-4. Real-estate growth for US regional markets, 2004–2007. Adaptation of chart © 2017 Economist.com.

Obviously, things were going well.

Making the Call

Here's what it was like to make the most terrifying – and most rewarding – call of my career.

Heading across London to the CNBC Europe television studios in March of 2007, I had no intention of predicting the collapse of the global economy.

My interview on *Power Lunch* had already been carefully organized, and my job that day was to explain how the US Federal Reserve had completely lost control over the American economy. If that were true, the world's largest economic engine was suddenly running without anyone at the wheel, and the results could be catastrophic.

That damage could start in the US and quickly overtake all of its trading partners, leaving almost no financially important country on the globe undamaged.

What could be worse?

Well, things can always get worse.

As the cab got closer to the studio, my thoughts were focused on a different issue – a mysterious broken pattern in global finance that had me at a loss. It was right at the edge of the US situation I'd planned to discuss, but this was much bigger.

Keep it simple, I thought: live television doesn't like complexity, or even two competing answers. Just state the problem clearly and be on your way – that would be best. With luck, I'd be back at my quarters in Home House – the club where our annual SNS London Dinner would be held later that evening – by 1 o'clock, with plenty of time to prepare for my dinner talk on global economics.

Since almost everyone in the markets was making money – and a lot of it – on the face of things, the timing of these concerns was way off. This message about the Fed losing its core operating ability was not being well-received by any of the press. Rather, the reverse seemed true. Until his recent retirement, Chairman Alan Greenspan had been the darling of the analysts. They seemed to think he walked on water, as they picked apart each of his finely crafted speeches with a care for detail usually reserved for some missing final chapter in a great religious text.

As far as I could tell, Greenspan had really blown it: he'd done a lot of damage to the markets – intentionally, at minimum, and perhaps illegally – and before his departure, the Fed had utterly lost control of the nation's economy. Although he'd been replaced by Ben Bernanke, the harm had been done, interest rates were effectively at zero, and commercial banks had stopped paying attention to the Fed altogether.

But right in the midst of worrying about this problem, something else captured my attention. Typically, it started as a small story

– discovered, in this case, in a newspaper over breakfast. Some of the world's equity markets had recently taken a small dip – not an uncommon event.

But a second read raised additional red flags. While the story couldn't have been more than a few paragraphs long, it turned out that *many* equity markets had declined – at the same time. Well, this was a well-known pattern, one we usually see in cases of large international news: the failure of a central bank, the pope getting shot.

But there was a problem: there was no such story, nothing that would shake many markets at once. Now there were suddenly two new issues to resolve. First, this was a "pattern broken," something that didn't normally happen and which didn't fit patterns I'd seen before. Second, it was bigger than it looked.

So, here was the gigantic new challenge: at the end of February 2007, most of the world's largest stock markets took a dive – all at once, at exactly the same time, for no apparent reason – and then (don't blink) they recovered. The amount of dip per country market wasn't huge – in the 2% to 5% range – but the fact that these events happened simultaneously, and the amount of money involved, was mind-blowing.

Here are a few charts depicting the moment:

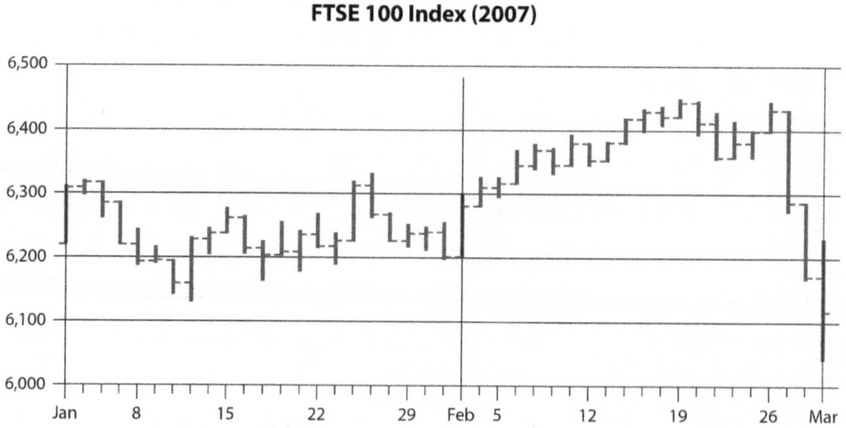

FTSE 100 Index (2007)

Figure 16-5. Performance of UK's FTSE, January 3–March 1, 2007. © 2017 MarketWatch (Bigcharts.com).

CAC 40 Index (2007)

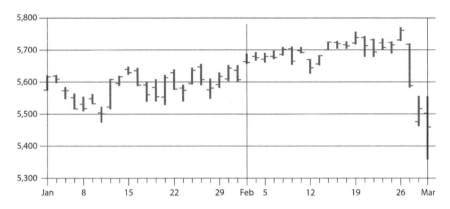

Figure 16-6. The French CAC, January 3, 2007–March 1, 2007. © 2017 MarketWatch (Bigcharts.com).

Dow Jones Industrial Average (2007)

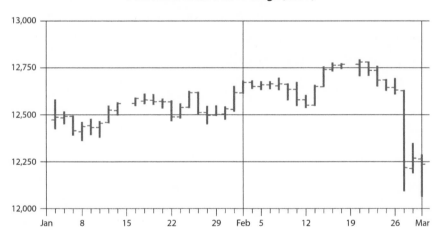

Figure 16-7. The DJIA, January 3, 2007–March 1, 2007. © 2017 MarketWatch (Bigcharts.com).

The DAX (2007)

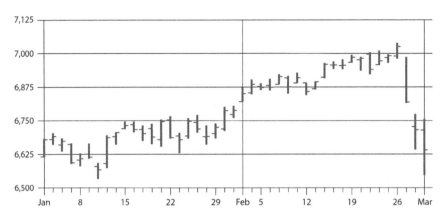

Figure 16-8. The German DAX, January 3, 2007–March 1, 2007. © 2017 MarketWatch (Bigcharts.com).

The data shown in the charts above may seem like a big drop when viewed over two months, but here's how small it was over the larger course of market patterns. Below are the same data, but taken from 2003 through the date of the call:

The DAX

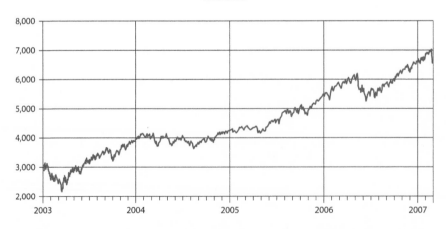

Figure 16-9. The German DAX, January 3, 2003–March 1, 2007. © 2017 MarketWatch (Bigcharts.com).

Clearly, the pattern wasn't in any particular stock over longer time sweeps, but in the behavior of all of them as a group.

It was as if one February Friday morning at 9am, the level of all of the oceans on the planet had dropped by six inches.

Just a few days after this small stock dive, funds mostly flowed back again, with markets returning to near former levels. Most people perceived this as the end of the story, and they were no doubt glad of it. Why worry about something that was already history?

But if you move through the world seeing patterns, it doesn't work that way.

Here was the broken pattern: If, say, Russia's or Italy's market goes up or down that much, no worries. If every stock market in the world does it at the same time, and it's because of a new world war or a global plague, it's a big deal, but it's not a pattern-breaker. But if almost every stock market in the world goes down 2% to 5% simultaneously, for no reason you can find on the front page of the *Financial Times*, the *New York Times*, or the *Wall Street Journal* – well, that's a pattern broken. It never happens – or rather, it had never happened before the last week of February 2007.

Traders are used to money sloshing around the world, from market to market, but for the whole equities pool to be drained, worldwide, all at once – this would have to involve a massive amount of money, and it suggested a process that was not obvious. How could it happen? Why *would* it happen?

This was a broken pattern of such importance that there had to be a serious explanation, and it was more than likely that, when unveiled, the news would not be good.

Because of the numbers involved, "massive" would have to mean on the scale of nation-sized, so big as to be beyond the control of any single person or group – or even all but a very few of the wealthiest nations. Few, if any, countries in the world had the power to move markets in this way, and fewer had the means to do it.

The *Financial Times* suggested that global investors might have been reacting to a change in Chinese commercial bank reserves, which had just been reset by the government of China.

This seemed laughable.

First, because these banks were so small in their interactions with global investors, there was very little connection between the two. Equity markets outside China and domestic Chinese banks had almost no intersection. Sure, investors get nervous when the Chinese telegraph larger problems by adjusting reserve rates, but there's too much of a gap between "nervous" and a global rout to make sense of this.

Second, Chinese banks aren't real banks; they're just state-owned and state-controlled pipes the government has been using for years to distribute cash to preferred companies and industries. Who cares about a few-percent shift in a rate that isn't part of any market, domestic or global?

Clearly, this explanation by the *Financial Times* was just a shot in the dark – and sure enough, a few days later the paper recanted and was looking elsewhere for a cause. I suddenly found myself in a financial detective race with the *FT*, for what turned out to be perhaps the most important economic call in history.

When our cab pulled into the studio lot, my PR "handler," Louise, and I headed through security to the green room to get mic'd up and wait for the nod to go onstage.

Who in the world could have caused all of that money to suddenly flow out of global stock markets? No king or queen had that much power.

First Go Deep, Then Go Forward

When I started using patterns to see the world differently, I realized there were two steps involved.

First go deep, then go forward.

Use patterns to understand how the world works in the present. Then you can move forward to follow those same patterns over time, which will help you make accurate predictions about the future.

It turns out that one of the results of studying the patterns of the world is you learn how it actually works – not how it's "supposed to" work, or how you or I or our parents wish it worked, and not how textbooks may have taught us it works. The patterns of the world are real, separate from emotion and opinion; they're part of the world as its wheels turn. When you learn from those turnings, you end up learning more about what's truly going on.

That is a simple, but profound, difference from how most people see the world around them.

But it makes sense: to accurately predict the future, you have to understand how the world works in the present.

The Role of the Bank of Japan

Two decades of watching currencies had convinced me that there were very few countries that could move that much money – literally trillions of dollars – overnight. In fact, the list was remarkably short: the Saudis, the Japanese, and maybe one or two others.

There was one good reason to start by looking at Japan: there were more broken patterns coming out of the Tokyo financial system. First, the governor of the Bank of Japan was politically at odds with the ruling LDP Party on a crucial issue relating to the setting of interest rates – a pattern-breaker I'd never seen before, and an important one.

Another broken pattern: It turned out that this new bank head had declared a half-point (.50 %) hike in interest rates, contrary to the wishes of his own party. More important (and un-Japanese), he did so without any advance warning to the outside world. At the time, the effective Japanese lending rate was essentially zero.

I'd been watching this rate for a few years. Most "normal" nations among the world's more advanced economies were enforcing rates in the area of 4% or higher. How could Japan get away with zero for so long?

Zero: it's just a weird number in the banking business. How can you make money at zero? It means that anyone in the know can borrow funds for free and not pay the bank any interest.

For savvy global investors, this was a tremendous opportunity: borrow at zero (in Japanese yen), convert to any other currency, and invest at whatever you can get, perhaps 5% or better. If you had the skills and stomach for this so-called "carry trade," it was a no-brainer. Who wouldn't want to do it?

The problem, as far as I could tell, was that no one in the global business world had a good understanding of the size of Japan's "carry trade." Was it large enough to qualify as the cause of the February financial earthquake? No one, not even the *FT*, knew.

I've been in a lot of TV-station green rooms in my time, and they're all different, and all the same. But green rooms for live national business television are unique, insofar as they're usually within eye contact of the stage, have glass walls instead of being windowless, and are very, very busy.

They're actually kind of fun – you often meet interesting people while they, too, wait their turns to go on camera. At any given moment, someone's just coming off the stage, someone's coming back from makeup, and someone else is waiting to go on. There is always a producer scurrying around with headphones and a wireless microphone, making sure there are no mistakes. Everything is fast and a bit tense, and there's almost no room for error.

The assumption is that you and the anchorperson both know at least the subject of what you're going to talk about. The anchors on these shows are impressive for their ability to keep it all together: they have one or two screens they're working from, but which they shouldn't appear to be looking at; they usually have a written script, which they consult during commercial breaks; and they're constantly interviewing new people, with only a few seconds to chat with them before the cameras come back on in a live broadcast.

On this day, a couple of young London entrepreneurs and their handler had joined me in the green room. Things were getting busier, and the countdown was down to a few minutes. I mentally walked through the three or four simple ideas about the Fed that flowed naturally from one to the another: The Fed had failed by attacking the Nasdaq at a time of no inflation. The Fed had contributed to the 2000 market crash. The banks had stopped keeping their loans and now cared only about instant fees on origination. The Fed rates no longer dictated these banks' lending rates. It would all sound logical, to those who were following these things.

But I was making progress on the Japanese question, and it had become clear where to look for the next clues.

Closing In on the Answer

The government of Japan had spent the last 15 years intervening in the currency markets for yen and dollars. I knew how important this was to technology companies, and I just happened to have had a nearly perfect record of accurate predictions in the ever-changing yen/dollar ratio. This wasn't because I understood the highly complex global free-currency markets, but rather because of the opposite: I'd figured out that this market was definitely not free. It was tightly constrained by ranges the government of Japan had been setting, and by direct market interventions by the Bank of Japan to enforce these ratios.

In other words, every time the market went against Japanese exporters and their desires, the government would intervene to correct the "problem."

I'd also looked into the currency ratio during the time of the equity earthquakes and felt a shock of excitement. If investors were diving back into the yen in their panic over the central bank's announcements, it would drive up the value of the yen, given that more buyers in any market drives prices higher. And if the Bank of Japan was true to form, it would intervene and try to push the value back down. Hopefully, there would be some evidence left behind, some public footsteps left in the market records.

There were two spikes in the chart for those few days in February – clear evidence of a classic intervention scenario – and one that had failed. Some entity, almost certainly the Bank of Japan, had come into the market twice, trying to stem the rise of the yen against the dollar, and had twice failed. You could palpably feel the struggle hidden in the abrupt peaks and valleys of this currency ratio.

In the language of Wall Street, the Japanese government had finally "capitulated." The traders' adage "You can't fight the market" is particularly true when dealing with global currency markets, where overnight trade volumes can reach $6 trillion or more, easily overwhelming even national central banks. The Japanese had spent a vast amount of money, for nothing.

Now I felt like I was closing in on an answer, because this ratio was at the heart of the mysterious carry trade. Global investors unwinding their borrowings would have to first reconvert into yen, pushing up its value.

So, how big was all this? Big enough to explain the simultaneous drop in global equity markets?

The Japanese government had spent about $350 billion the prior year – 2006 – doing these interventions, and I'd already predicted that they'd roughly double that budget in 2007. If this first prediction was correct, they would have set aside about $600–$700 billion for the year, continuing a pattern of market intervention and increased spending on the issue.

This would be the Bank of Japan's lever in the intervention: trying to move the "stone" of a fast-rising yen.

It made sense to assume that after raising the interest rate, the Japanese themselves had been so shocked when the yen took off that they'd gone into panic mode. How much would that mean they might have spent on an intervention? Maybe up to half the year's budget, or around $300 billion, all at once? This was strictly a guess, but it was my best guess, and at least it helped get me into rounding-error territory.

Now that I knew roughly the size of the lever, I could guess at the weight of the stone.

How much money must have been flowing through the Japanese carry trade in those few days if $300 billion was able to move the needle, but not block the momentum in yen appreciation for more than a few minutes?

By now, the *FT* had publicly proposed that the carry trade totaled about $250 billion, and so was too small to be the culprit.

But perhaps the *FT* had made a serious mistake by underestimating the size of the carry trade. If it was really only $250 billion, then the Bank of Japan would've won its battle by spending what it had. Indeed, if the bank's estimated $300 billion spent in that short time could move the carry trade only slightly, then the total flow had to be much – *much* – larger.

How much larger?

This required another reach. Because the bank's spending had caused at least temporary spikes in the yen/dollar ratio, I guessed that the opposing funds flow was at least three to four times larger, at minimum. How about $1 trillion? In fact, how about something like $1T-plus?

(A few months later, I was to learn that the actual number, according to a new *FT* study, was about $3 trillion.)

This was the answer I was looking for. If the unannounced actions of the Bank of Japan had caused a sudden reversal of the flow through the carry trade, we might have seen a shift of $1T-plus in global investment funds. An actual reversal of that size would mean a potential effect on equity markets of even more than that amount, since many investors were highly leveraged.

And that was enough, or was at least in the right range, to explain the February market earthquake.

What's That Smell?

It was as I walked onto the CNBC *Power Lunch* stage that it finally hit me:

The mistake of a bank functionary in Tokyo had apparently just caused a terrifying shock to nearly all of the world's equity markets. Wow!

What did that mean?

Global investors had panicked when the Japanese threatened their source of free funds. They'd been forced to pull money out of stocks and send it back through Japan. Who knew what this crazy guy at the Bank of Japan might do next? Double down?

When the bank later publicly reassured them that there would be no more unannounced increases, investors took a breath, looked around, and put their money right back where it had been before.

And then came the truly frightening wake-up call. What this *really* meant was there was far too much global liquidity, too much "hot money," running around the world looking for overnight investments. Money that earlier had been residing in stable, long-term investments (say, bonds, certificates of deposit, or other long-term holdings) had been recycled through Tokyo for short-term, higher-margin returns.

It meant that anything, almost any bad thing at all, could now cause an economic disaster.

I felt like I was standing at the door of a gigantic dark, empty warehouse. That funny smell was coming from gasoline, which covered the entire floor as far as I could see in the gloom. And someone had just lit a cigarette at the far end of the room.

Breaking the News

As I settled into my chair on *Power Lunch* to talk about how the Federal Reserve had lost control of the US economy, it was suddenly clear that the economy of the whole world was at risk.

The producer did the countdown, and a tall, well-dressed, all-business anchor – we'll call her "Renee" – turned and introduced me:

"And today, we have Mark Anderson, the CEO of the Strategic News Service, here to tell us why he thinks the Fed has lost control of the US economy. His readers include Bill Gates, Michael Dell, and many of today's leaders in technology and finance. Mark?"

Even my original message was going to be tough to get across: anyone who knew how things worked in the global economy would be shocked at the thought that there was no engineer at the front of the American economic train. It was a pretty terrifying idea.

I quickly described the Fed's problems – how it had taken on too many tasks, how commercial banking had changed, and how banks had detached themselves from the kinds of profits that used to give the Fed its control over them.

A few years earlier, banks would've moved in lockstep with the Fed: if the Fed raised rates a quarter point, so did the banks – both in the US and Canada, generally – within minutes or hours. But now, with fees being the banks' only real concern, the Fed could push rates one way and the banks could ignore it, or even go in the opposite direction, which some did. Worse, the Fed had driven interest rates to essentially zero, in an ill-advised desire to suck money out of the equity markets – which was not in its charter in any case. This gave the Fed no more room to lower rates; it was out of bullets.

I concluded by saying that the Fed had lost control of the banks, and so, to a large degree, of the US economy.

Renee seemed surprised, but satisfied. Fresh new ideas, great stuff, right on schedule. I think she also knew how really frightening this was, but she had her own trains to run.

"There is one more thing we might discuss," I suggested. Her expression changed ever so slightly: going off-script is almost never good, especially on live TV.

"What is it? Another prediction?" She was pretending to be excited, but I could hear the concern in her voice.

I was taking a huge risk. My revelation was too big to ignore, but if it was wrong, I'd never hear the end of it. It would be Predictions Suicide, live at noon.

And there was no time to think it over properly. Everything was happening in real time.

"Yes, it's something I've been working on this week. It appears that global liquidity levels have gotten so vast that the world economic system is extremely vulnerable to a collapse. Almost any shock could trigger it."

For a moment she seemed to lose her composure; her face went blank as she sat staring at me. I tried to imagine what she was thinking: "How dare you bring this crazy idea to my show!" But just as quickly she regained her cool, and the feeling moved to something more like, "Did we just break the story of the century?" As far as I could tell, the latter, if the prediction was correct, was true.

"And what would you recommend our viewers do with their investments?"

There was no time to think of any kind of investment advice, even though the need was obvious. I had to resort to a standby rule that has never failed me: When you don't know something, say so.

"I really don't know," I confessed. If only Renee had known how little time I'd had to think about *all* of this, she would've been doubly shocked. "I suspect that going into cash might be the best move."

Shortly thereafter, I was thanked, led offstage, and arrived back in the hustle of the green room. The producer came in and thanked me, as a quiet little voice in the back of my head was saying, "Did you really just put that out, on live international television?" Might as well go out in a ball of fire . . .

Someone removed the mic from my collar, and I picked up my coat. "How long will you be in London?" the producer asked. "We'd love to have you back."

When I suggested the weekend, she apologized: "We never have the same guest back during the same week. No exceptions. Company rules. But come by next time you are in London." I was thinking about how polite the British are when you've just committed hara-kiri in public on their stage.

Louise and I thanked her and started down the corridor, when there was a sudden commotion behind us: a runner had come from the stage area and was whispering in the producer's ear. She nodded and walked over to us.

"Renee would like you back with us on Friday, if you can make it," the producer said. She seemed a bit startled. "She wants to talk with you more about this collapse." Apparently, we were about to break house rules.

"We'll be here," I told her.

The world had been warned. Next we'd see if anyone was paying attention, and what, if anything, they would do about it. As we walked back to the taxi, Louise and I were both silent. "That was rather amazing," she said suddenly, with an enthusiastic smile. I nodded.

The global economy was running at a breathtaking, historic pace that day. It was even sunny in London as we drove back to the club.

Five months later, the greatest economic collapse in world history began to unfold. The cigarette had hit the warehouse floor.

Those of us who got this right were all looking at flows, and the patterns within them.

Chapter 17

Calling the Oil Price Collapse

As difficult as it was to predict the Global Financial Collapse, there's another economic prediction of which I'm equally proud – the collapse of the global oil price. The global price of oil, and its sudden decline, is the single most important commodity input in the world economy. Everything needs energy, oil is the most common form of it, and its price acts like a tax on virtually all of the world's goods and services.

The Oil Price Collapse radically rearranged the geopolitical and economic status of almost every country in the world, and virtually every analyst and national leader was caught by surprise when it happened.

Here's what Saudi Prince Alwaleed bin Talal said in a *USA Today* interview with Maria Bartiromo about being able to see this coming:

Q: Can you explain Saudi Arabia's strategy in terms of not cutting oil production?

A: Saudi Arabia and all of the countries were caught off guard. No one anticipated it was going to happen. *Anyone who says they anticipated this 50% drop [in price] is not saying the truth.* [Emphasis mine.]

Because the minister of oil in Saudi Arabia just in July publicly said $100 is a good price for consumers and producers. And less than six months later, the price of oil collapses 50%.[1]

But the prince – one of the world's great investors – was wrong. And the secret to getting this call right was in following not just one thread of the usual price patterns, but three other pattern trends.

Perhaps it would help to put the call into perspective using a pricing chart.

This is my prediction, from our *SNS Global Report* on October 2, 2014 [emphasis mine]:

Peak Pricing, Not Peak Oil

SNS was probably the first to debunk the latest "Peak Oil" cry of *Wolf!*, catching the trend within days, if not hours. Aren't you glad you aren't the author of that book?

Today, the world is seeing falling oil prices, even as war rages on in the Middle East. This has given some traders pause, as they are used to the tried and true "bullets = bucks" equation for one of the many ways cartels, and traders, keep the prices moving, and going up. Some New York traders are even wondering if, this time, it's different.

It is.

The advent of fracking, and new oil discoveries on- and offshore, have fundamentally changed the psychology – and the ground truth – of the oil market. No one wants to deal with the Middle East anymore, and no one really needs to. The OPEC cartel is essentially no longer a cartel, having lost its corner on the market long ago. And the press forward with alternative energies is not good news for the oil lobby.

---

[1] Maria Bartiromo, "Saudi Prince: $100-a-Barrel Oil 'Never' Again," *USA Today* (Jan. 11, 2015), https://www.usatoday.com/story/money/columnist/bartiromo/2015/01/11/bartiromo-saudi-prince-alwaleed-oil-100-barrel/21484911.

Just ask the Rockefeller family how they feel. Having been publicly rebuked a few years ago by management of the company they founded, and in which they were still the largest shareholders, they are this week divesting from all fossil fuel firms, including climate-change denier ExxonMobil. In a statement, they noted they would be investing in alternative energy sources going forward.

I've long said that the real price of oil – meaning, the cost of getting it out of the ground plus making a reasonable (vs. rapacious) profit – is in the $14/bbl range. With increased costs for difficulty of retrieval (deeper wells and waters) and more advanced technology, that price should be higher; perhaps it's $45–$55 today.

Here's a quick look at where prices are going:

Crude Oil WTI – Monthly Continuation Candlestick Chart

While a chartist might see the end of this fall somewhere around $90/bbl, I am suggesting that we have much further to go.

$50/bbl should do it. How long will it take? Since I think China is hitting a real set of economic blocks, I am expecting this to be sooner, rather than later; perhaps 5 years or less, rather than 10.

And since this will change almost everything in global economics, it seems worth sharing with our members.

I don't think oil is ever coming back.[2]

The first thing a Wall Street analyst would have seen in the above chart (made at the time of the call) is that it shows what seems like a long-term upward trend in oil prices; that was true.

Now, looking back, the suggestion that the real price of oil should be between $45 and $55 per barrel, and that it would drop to $50, looks rather prescient:

The Oil Price Collapse

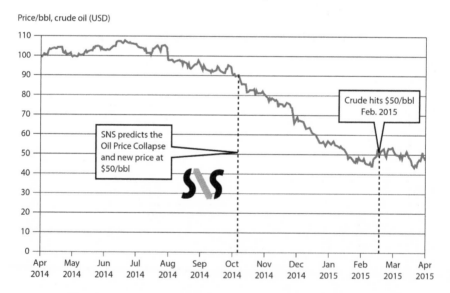

Figure 17-1. Oil Price Collapse of 2015, as predicted by SNS. Data source: Energy Information Administration.

---

[2] Mark R. Anderson, "Peak Pricing, Not Peak Oil," *SNS Global Report*, 17:37, October 2, 2014.

Here's the same chart, updated, with pricing in black and volatility in grey:

Crude Oil Price and Price Volatility

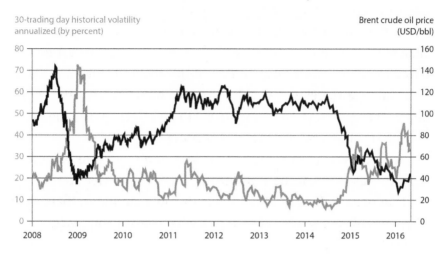

Figure 17-2. Crude oil price volatility, January 1, 2008–May 2, 2016. Data from Energy Information Administration.

One of the noticeable long-term reads on this eight-year picture is that oil prices were almost rock-steady in a band between 100 and 125 or so from January 2011 to September 2014. Even when the price dipped into the $93 range (the price when I made our call), the market had seen that price and returned higher twice before in recent times, and price volatility was at a record low.

In other words, there wasn't anything in the charts of the time to suggest a sudden price collapse.

How Did I Make the Call?

I was watching four major trends at once, three of which I mentioned in the prediction. Let's take those first:

1. Fracking. *The advent of fracking, and new oil discoveries on- and offshore, have fundamentally changed the psychology – and the ground truth – of the oil market. No one wants to deal with the Middle East any more, and no one really needs to.*

The practice of fracking had come out of nowhere to profoundly change the oil and gas business. This was bound to have a double effect on oil prices, since: a) oil that people had thought was hard to find, and was therefore valuable, was turning up all over the world; and b) the same was even more true of natural-gas wells, and every kilocalorie of natural-gas energy was going to replace oil.

The result was imminent, and obvious: if a long-term pattern of scarcity was about to be replaced by producing wells everywhere, the traditional price would not hold. The only questions, then, were when the collapse would occur and to what new pricing levels.

2. The End of OPEC Cartel Pricing Power. *The OPEC cartel is essentially no longer a cartel, having lost its corner on the market long ago.*

Saudi Arabia had long controlled the OPEC cartel, and the patterns around its power and its use had become reliable. A long series of recent OPEC meetings had led from the old patterns of the Saudis dictating control of prices, through forced agreement on production cutbacks among members, to a lack of discipline, with members either refusing openly or agreeing but not performing.

Just as important, the Saudi royal family had become used to high oil prices, leading them to profligate spending. While they used to do well when oil was $14/bbl, their spending had grown so fast that it was estimated they needed to see $100 oil just to pay their bills every year. This suggested that they couldn't cut back themselves, even if they threatened to do so. After years of propping up prices, they'd run out of tricks and tools to continue the charade.

For all these reasons, their power to control OPEC had become a myth, and with the removal of OPEC from the pricing discussion, there was nothing to resist a collapse.

3. Global Warming and the Rise of Alternative Energy Sources. *The press forward with alternative energies is not good news for the oil lobby.*

If the first two of these pattern trends were relatively large and immediate, the world's scientific acceptance of global warming was much greater in effect, and obviously was going to last beyond our lifetimes. Its most important result: after decades of not caring about replacements for oil (except to avoid wars), every nation on Earth was gearing up its political, scientific, and business wills in an all-out effort to find alternative sources to burning fossil fuels. While the US coal and oil lobbies lied to the public and did their best to emulate the tobacco lobby's old "Nicotine is not addictive" public-relations campaign, it was clear that global warming was real, was becoming generally accepted as human-caused, and would continue.

The results would also, therefore, be as stark as they were new: a rush into wind, solar, and other alternative energies, which would not cease until the last oil-fired (and coal-fired and gas-fired) plant was shuttered.

This downward pricing pressure would be as inexorable as the warming trend itself.

While these three patterns were sufficient to make the call, there were even more clues of a sudden drop. Iraq was likely to soon increase oil pumping by a large margin, and Iran would be coming back into the market behind it. Both were major oil producers, so the pressure on prices would be even more relentless on the supply side.

And, on the demand side, things were already going south: the world's ability to store extra oil was almost exhausted. Everyone wanted to sell, and fewer wanted to buy, filling the US strategic storage system to nearly 100% capacity.

What would happen when all the tanks were full? Producers would have to sell at any price.

So much for the drop itself, and the timing. But what about the final price? Even today, I will admit that I'm amazed I got that right. Perhaps it was just dumb luck.

I had spent years studying the oil business. One of the most important patterns in oil pricing, I'd discovered, was not about the oil coming out of the ground, but the price manipulation available to the big oil firms. This is a story probably still not well told even today, but those who followed the Enron debacle will have some idea of the process. Fraudulent shutdowns of refineries at just the wrong (right) time drove up prices when needed. Reported problems in ethanol mixing, and in meeting other government requirements, were used to price advantage.

It seemed that every complication and delay somehow just went straight down into a plus for the bottom line. The number and types of schemes used to create high oil prices – and high company profits – were both outrageous and ongoing. The system was ripe for a fall.

When the most recent call for "peak oil" had come out, suggesting that oil production would decline from then on, I was able to debunk it within hours, although plenty of stock and commodity investors got taken in. When the manipulators got prices up near $150 per barrel using the fake justification of peak oil, I was able to call the peak price within a couple of dollars and get both the number and the timing right.

In other words, there were plenty of historic patterns of pricing and behavior available to anyone who was watching, almost always linked to some form of fraud or intentional pseudo-problem. In this sense, it helped to have an intuitive sense of price.

When the oil-sands business started up in Alberta, the cost of producing a barrel had jumped into the $23 range at the time; I was also aware that, since those early days, it had gone considerably higher.

So, knowing that the price had nowhere to go but down, and that it was going to happen sooner rather than later – and seeing a large and increasing batch of pressures aligning against the price – the only question was one of degree. Would it drop a few dollars? No, not with these irrevocable issues in the way.

Clearly, it wouldn't be allowed to go to zero. What was the real production cost in modern times? While this was a closely kept secret (and not to be confused with what Big Oil was saying), it seemed to me that something just slightly higher than the tar-sands production cost would make sense. If it had doubled since the inception of those fields, based on the usual economics of size and waste, the cost would be about $46. And that's how I made the call.

As we now know (see Figures 17-1 and 17-2 on pages 188–189), the initial collapse took the price down from about $95 average to about $50, and then $45.

It was a good day for the countries and companies of the world that could stop paying this ridiculous "oil tax."

As you can guess from Figure 17-1, this was not an easy prediction to make; the usual patterns all argued against it. But by following the patterns of what really mattered, instead of what appeared on the Wall Street pricing charts, I became the only person to get it right publicly.

Even today, it's hard to imagine how much money was lost by those who didn't see this coming, or how much might have been made by those who did – but the figure has to be in the trillions of dollars.

Chapter 18

Calling the China Crash

I first became interested in China's national business model – how China makes money as a country – soon after it moved away from Maoism and toward the Japanese model. Having watched Japan manipulate its currency for decades in order to win in trade relations with the outside world, I felt an internal alarm go off when China adopted the same plan.

If Japan could wreak havoc on its trading partners as a small country with an outsized economy, what would happen if China moved to the same illegal and unfair practices? The result couldn't be good.

As China's patterns of economic behavior began to fall in line with Japan's, I started looking more deeply into not only currency manipulation, but also all the other practices of what we eventually named the "InfoMerc," or infomercantilist, model. Structural barriers were going up to keep competitors at bay, subsidies for export companies were going up, and, most important, the theft of foreign crown-jewel intellectual property (IP) – the "secret sauce" of Western businesses – was being stolen at an alarming, and rapidly increasing, rate.

While Deng Xiaoping was declaring that "it is glorious to be rich," the Communist Party was adopting measures that would ensure it, with outright theft and fraud as the cornerstones of the new five-year plans.

After five years of accelerating research and increasing levels of alarm at the actions (as opposed to the words) of the Communist Party planners, it seemed clear there was a real problem – one that would require a huge increase in my own time and energy. China had decided on a path of IP theft that amounted to economic warfare: the Party planners had adopted, and modified, a system that had only one intended result.

The purpose of its updated InfoMerc model was asymmetric trade on a global scale, ensuring that exports exceeded imports and that all trading partners would be impoverished, transaction by transaction. But more important, it included stealing the world's critical trade secrets, from CEO emails on pricing to chip blueprints and factory processes.

The goal of most military wars is to gain economic domination, but the Chinese didn't want or need war – just the opposite, in fact. They needed peace, so that they could gain economic domination using their new model without a shot being fired.

Going to the Masters

I spent a few years writing about different aspects of China's model and about my concerns, and then decided to take my work and conclusion to those who knew best. Over the next six months, I briefed senior personnel in the offices that seemed most likely to know, or need to know, about the problem. In the US, these included top officials at the White House, the State Department, the Commerce Department, the NSA, the FBI, the Department of Justice, the CIA, the US Trade Department, and the Department of Homeland Security, among others. Overseas, this included top officers of government in Australia and, in Britain, the heads of GCHQ, MI5, MI6, the Cabinet Minister's Office, and others.

No one disagreed; all of them thanked me, and were glad to have the information.

Rather than feeling relief, I came away much more concerned: if *I* was briefing *them*, there was a hell of a lot more work to be done.

From that point on, my research became much more intense, and the findings much more worrying. In one project, for example, we looked at the Chinese banking system. The state said it owned only four of the top 10 banks. We published proof that it owned or fully controlled 10 out of 10. In later work, we found that the entire banking system was fraudulent, with fake accounting and endless bad loans. The banks were nothing but pipes for distributing cash based on Party preferences. When the cash disappeared, which it inevitably did, an email from the Party was enough to fill the coffers again.

I'll never forget the moment when pattern after pattern of fraud and illegal behavior finally gelled into a clear picture. We had just seen the emergence of a criminal state, one that made up to half of its money through theft and fraud.

It was almost unbelievable. How could a country the size of China get away with this? The answer was visible in a pattern of lies and deceit, combined with the world's most structured and most effective regime of propaganda, censorship, and social repression. No one outside China – or perhaps even outside the Party Standing Committee – was supposed to know how China really made money.

At SNS, we created a white paper with another year's worth of research, funded by us and fellow corporate leaders willing to help put a stop to these practices. We worked with *60 Minutes* to create what became perhaps the most-watched investigative segment in the show's history ("The Great Brain Robbery," with Leslie Stahl). And we briefed all of the global leaders, again, with our new findings, on exactly how the Chinese national model worked. The Department of Justice said we had created the most complete description to date of the Chinese national business model.

Given all of this theft and fraud, it began to strike me that something would have to give at some point. If you take the seven very smart (and mostly foreign-educated) men on the Standing Committee and try to prop up a fraudulent national scheme decade after decade, an interesting thing is likely to happen. The facts of their absolute power, extensive training, and high intelligence meant two things: first, that they could pull this off for much longer than most people, hiding a small mountain of problems and failures from outsiders and even from their own citizens, whose unrest they feared more than anything else; and second, that when the house of cards finally came down, it would come down at a dramatic pace.

The pattern of outward calm by the Party broke on or about January 1, 2015. A flurry of flawed maneuvers and inappropriate announcements telegraphed that the Standing Committee had likely just been briefed by their top internal economists that things were going badly awry, and that it was time for any and all emergency measures. These were now being put into place.

For almost six months, the signs remained muted, but problems almost certainly continued to mount. Sometime in the first two weeks of May, it looked as though a second emergency meeting of the same type had occurred. This time, if patterns of behavior were to be believed, the news from the internal economists must've been even worse, likely reporting that the most extreme efforts had had little or no effect. At this meeting, Committee members must have felt doomed. The realization of their greatest fear – that a publicly known economic downturn would lead to Party overthrow – seemed, in that case, almost inevitable.

Soon after, the world caught on. The Shanghai market, and then other Chinese markets, imploded. The yuan began to collapse, just after a gullible Christine Legarde allowed it into the IMF basket of official currency reserves.

One major pattern break occurred at around this time, as the Chinese risked losing their bid to bring the yuan into the IMF (a top national priority) in order to move back to fraudulently cheapening their currency – because, it seemed, they were so terrified of the impending economic collapse. They were acting as though they had no other options.

When country leaders betray a top national priority, you know there's an even more important reason than meets the eye. It was this pattern broken that led to our second warning to the public of China's imminent economic collapse.

The following January, just before our annual Washington state Predictions event, one of the technology leaders in the crowd stood up. "Mark Anderson told us that China was going to collapse, and I called my broker and got us out of all of our exposures to China. He saved my family's investments."

China's self-inflicted troubles continue to mount today, but hopefully we were able to warn enough people that the damage from its practices has been reduced.

Only the future patterns will tell.

Epilogue

Many of the calls in this book sounded impossible, yet most of them are now part of history.

Finding Einstein's Biggest Mistake (not the one he first gave this name to, nor the one physics students have long been taught), and later learning that Einstein *himself* agreed – sounds like something from a fairytale. Finding a cause – and therefore potential cures through vaccines – for some cancers: it's not going to happen, right? Every chapter in this book describes something that a normal person would deem to be highly unlikely – probably for any group of people, and certainly for a single person from "outside" that category of expertise.

All of this comes from studying patterns in what I believe to be a new way.

The primary story of this book is that this ability is about the message, not the messenger. Any reasonably motivated person should be able to use these same tools to see the future clearly.

It turns out that by using pattern recognition, it's possible to know more about a country than its leader does, more about a company than its CEO does, more about science than trained scientists do, and more about economics than trained economists do. Why is this so? Because professional and academic training offered today covers everything except how to see what's really happening, how to find the patterns in something which are not only real, but which also point the way toward what to expect from a deeper, or longer, look.

Unlike humans, and even their books, patterns don't make mistakes, and patterns don't lie.

These stories of discovery are told as real-life, Sherlock Holmes–style detective tales, which is true to the rather thrilling (and high-stakes) experience of using patterns to find these amazing treasures.

My hope is that the challenge of making these discoveries will turn out to be the most exciting, fun experience you've ever had. I know that once you've learned to see patterns, and you've improved your skills at seeing ahead, how and what you see will be changed forever.

Appendix

Selected Successful SNS Calls

The following charts are intended to lend context to some of the most important SNS predictions.

The Oil Price Collapse

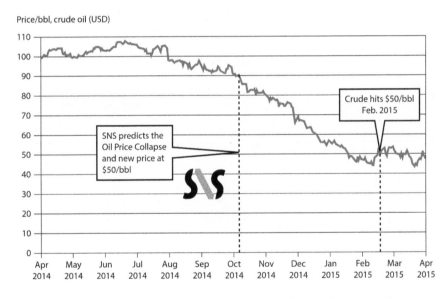

Figure A-1. SNS predicts the Oil Price Collapse of 2015. Data source: Energy Information Administration.

The CarryAlong PC

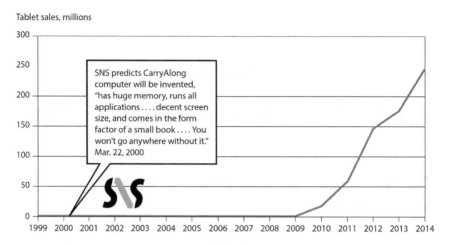

Figure A-2. SNS predicts the development and popularity of the "CarryAlong" computer.

The Global Financial Collapse

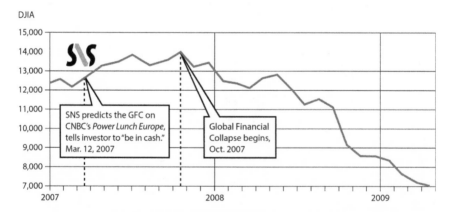

Figure A-3. SNS predicts the Global Financial Crisis of 2007.

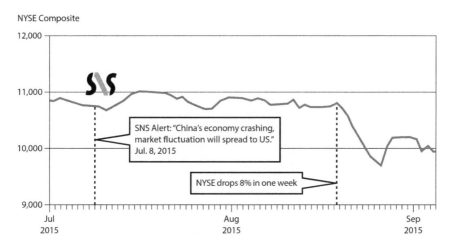

Figure A-4. SNS predicts the 2015 crash of the Chinese economy.

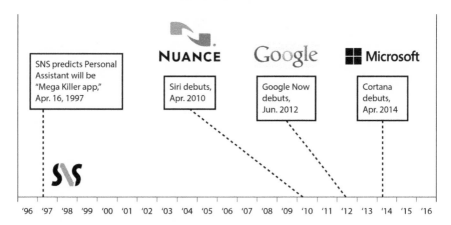

Figure A-5. In 1997, SNS predicts the development of personal-assistant apps such as Siri, Google Now, and Cortana.

Acknowledgments

This has been a long, challenging, and exciting journey, supported by family and friends for decades. My sincere thanks go out to my wife, Mary Jane, for being there throughout the voyage; to SNS editor-in-chief and this book's editor, Sally Anderson, and our publisher, Judith Bloch, for keeping me on whatever looks even slightly like the straight and narrow writing path; to Sharon Anderson Morris and Scott Schramke of SNS for keeping the wheels on our many shared ventures while all of this took place; to Evan Anderson and Berit Anderson for encouraging me to persevere in this very long effort; to Denyse Davis for holding all the pieces together despite my tendency toward chaos; and to all those in our companies and the SNS and FiRe tribes, who continue to be a critical part of this story. I look forward to our next steps together.

About the Author

Mark Anderson is CEO of Strategic News Service (SNS) and publisher of the weekly *SNS Global Report on Technology and the Global Economy* (www.stratnews.com), read by Bill Gates, Elon Musk, Vint Cerf, Michael Dell, Paul Allen, Craig Venter, Jeff Bezos, Bill Janeway, Paul Jacobs, Leroy Hood, and technology executives and investors worldwide. He is CEO of the SNS Conference Corp. and chairman of the Future in Review (FiRe) conference (www. futureinreview.com) – now in its 15th year – which *The Economist* has named "the best technology conference in the world." He is also the founding CEO of Coventry Computer, a startup in stealth mode.

Mark's work includes the creation of INVNT/IP (Inventing Nations vs. Nation-sponsored Theft of IP, www.invntip.com), a global consortium of corporations and government agencies; SNS Project Inkwell (www.projectinkwell.org), the first global consortium to bring vendors, educators, and students together to accelerate the deployment of appropriate technology into K-12 schools; SNS Interactive News (www.snsinews.com), using patented processes to bring daily interactive communications "About Leaders, For Leaders" worldwide; a new Global Rescue System (GRS) for victims of human trafficking, in concert with Julia Ormond's ASSET program; Orca

Relief Citizens' Alliance (ORCA: www.orcarelief.org), the sole non-profit organization working to reduce killer whale mortality rates; and Nutritional Microanalysis, a new field of medical research and practice aimed at connecting biochemical descriptions of food with health. The subscription-based SNS FiReFilms initiative (www.firefilms.net) was created in 2009 to identify, support, and promote potentially world-changing documentary films in which technology improves the human condition. SNS FiReBooks publishes books on how technology drives the global economy.

Mark is credited with accelerating the deployment of 3G wireless in Iceland; helping design Sweden's wireless auction process; assisting Eastern Germany's technology programs; creating Project Intelligent Response, the first post-911 manual for the US government on the use of technology to combat terror; and being the first to fully document the central role of stolen intellectual property in China's national business model. His successful predictions include the Great Financial Collapse of late 2007 (made in March of that year, on CNBC's *Power Lunch Europe*); the contemporary outbreak of "currency wars" and the first modern use of the term; the advent and success of the CarryAlong computer category as the fastest-growing and largest in the industry, now represented by pads and netbooks (in 1997); the first detailed description of the Internet Assistant category, currently represented by Siri, Google Now, and Dragon Go! (in 1998); and the global currency crisis of late 1997 (in April of that year) – leading to a publicly graded 94.5% prediction accuracy record since 1995. He is the only person to have publicly predicted both the Great Financial Collapse and the Oil Price Collapse, the two most important economic events of modern times.

Mark's intellectual contributions include Resonance Theory – the first physics Theory of Everything based on the resonant properties of empty space; the AORTA (Always-On Real-Time Access) concept, subsequently taken as the name for Europe's first broadband network; the AORTA Manifesto, a proven process for K-12 schools integrating technology, since adopted by the White House in its ConnectED initiative and by NGOs and educators around the world; Equilibrium Genetics, a new theory of evolution, cell function, and genetic variation; the Global Trifecta Proposal – a solution set to slow global warming, based on linking commercial graphene production to energy-plant CO_2 emissions and graphene 3D printing; and Flow Economics and Hyperstructural Economics, two new pragmatic descriptions of the forces behind the post-Information Age economy.

Mark is co-founder of the new Pattern Recognition Laboratory at UC San Diego, a member of the Australian American Leadership Dialogue, and an advisory board member of the Calit2 and Qualcomm Institutes, the Graphene Industry Stakeholders Assn. (GSA), and the GSA Center of Excellence. He provides advice to or has invested in Ignition Partners, Mohr Davidow Ventures, the Global Advisory Council of the mPedigree Network (Ghana), SwedeTrade, The Family Circle (Europe), the NSA, the Department of Justice, the FBI, the DHS, the NGA, the State Department, USTR, the White House, GCHQ, MI5, the British Cabinet Minister's Office, and industry-leading firms including Dell, Microsoft, Google, Symantec, Nuance Communications, and others. His work was recently showcased in the *60 Minutes* segment "The Great Brain Robbery," and he is a frequent guest on National Public Radio's *All Things Considered*, as well as the *BBC World News* and Bloomberg TV. He regularly appears in *The Economist*, the *Financial Times*, *The New York Times*, *The Wall Street Journal*, and other media.

Index

Page locators in *italics* indicate figures.